Understanding Popular Music

DAVID VENTURA

RHINEGOLD
EDUCATION

www.rhinegoldeducation.co.uk

Also available from Rhinegold Education:

GCSE, AS and A Level Music Study Guides (AQA, Edexcel and OCR)

GCSE, AS and A Level Music Listening Tests (AQA, Edexcel and OCR)

GCSE, AS and A Level Music Revision Guides (AQA, Edexcel and OCR)

AS/A2 Music Technology Study Guide (Edexcel)

AS/A2 Music Technology Listening Tests (Edexcel)

Key Stage 3 Listening Tests: Book 1 and Book 2

AS and A2 Music Harmony Workbooks

GCSE and AS Music Composition Workbooks

GCSE and AS Music Literacy Workbooks

Musicals in Focus, Baroque Music in Focus, Film Music in Focus

Music Technology from Scratch

Dictionary of Music in Sound

First published 2012 in Great Britain by

Rhinegold Education

14-15 Berners Street

London W1T 3LJ

www.rhinegoldeducation.co.uk

Understanding Popular Music

Order No. RHG401

ISBN: 978-1-78038-249-4

Exclusive Distributors:

Music Sales Ltd

Distribution Centre, Newmarket Road

Bury St Edmunds, Suffolk IP33 3YB, UK

Printed in the EU

Companion website:

www.hybridpublications.com

Access code: TR398

Contents

Introduction

There is a great deal of skill involved in the way pop music is put together and delivered by composers, performers and recording engineers. Understanding the music's cultural background, how it was composed and the studio production techniques employed together with appreciating the performance styles of the artists involved can enhance both the listening experience and the ability to produce one's own work. This book looks at some of the many different strands of pop music and, by selecting representative examples, unpicks the components that come together to form a pop song. The title, *Understanding Popular Music*, represents the knowledge that can be gained by adopting this approach. It covers more than sixty years of musical development and examines the various musical characteristics of the styles that emerged during that time. It can be argued that the roots of the genre go back further, even to the turn of the century cakewalks of Debussy or the music of the black slaves in the southern American states. *Grove Music Online* states that 'the term "pop music" originated in Britain in the mid-1950s as a description for Rock and Roll and the new youth music styles that it influenced …', and I have taken this as a starting point. The term 'Popular Music' is not used in its wider sense: it is not meant to be applied to all aspects of popular music such as easy listening or Classic FM's top playlists. Neither is it meant to be used in the way some academics define pop as a particular kind of commercial chart music. It includes pop charts, rock music, reggae, electronic dance and some crossover folk styles, and looks at these from a musical perspective selecting a number of examples of successful record releases to illustrate how they are put together.

The book is not meant to be comprehensive and I am acutely aware that some important artists are given short shrift or left out altogether. Reference books are available for the purposes of providing complete surveys. I have also tried to avoid high-level academic analysis and technical terminology, although a certain amount is indispensable, hopefully explained by the margin boxes that link to the keywords in the text that are highlighted in bold. Most selections are of singles rather than album tracks, although some album tracks are used when a particular style or technique needs to be demonstrated. The instruments used in pop music are featured at various places but only in the depth required for non-players to gain some understanding of how they work. Developments in music technology through the decades are given their own short sections and also referred to in the main text when they become essential to the style under examination.

Students taking GCSE music and A levels in music or music technology will find useful material within these pages. In fact, many of the examination set study pieces receive scrutiny and analysis within the chapters. However, the book is not intended for examination study alone but can be used by young people starting off in the pop music world seeking to enhance their songwriting by understanding the methods of commercially successful artists. Students on wider-based performing arts courses will also be able to draw relevant information for their researches.

It is not possible using words alone to convey the exact way some music is capable of putting across its message. Descriptive and analytical text can provide pointers to the student but it is always best to listen to the music that is being discussed. Therefore the publisher has put together a number of playlists and a companion website in order to provide audio accompaniment to the analysis. See the How to use this book pages for details.

I am indebted to my son Sebastian, who possesses an encyclopaedic knowledge of modern music from the last few decades and has provided helpful suggestions. I would also like to thank Emma Cooper, Commissioning Editor for Rhinegold Education, who has given much-needed support and encouragement throughout the writing process, and I am very grateful for the invaluable expertise of Tom Farncombe, who brought his experience with *Pop Music: The Text Book* to bear. A number of fellow music teachers and education colleagues have also contributed helpful advice on the book's contents. I would also like to thank Peter Fletcher, Nathan Scott, Chris Pratt and Louise Ventura for helping prepare the website audio clips.

David Ventura

How to use

A companion website supports this book with links to playlists and downloadable audio files.

Keywords in bold in the text are defined in margin boxes

This icon indicates that an audio example is available on the website

Swing: Music that swings has a bouncy character derived from subtle timing in the rhythms of notes against a regular beat. Listeners want to tap their feet or nod their heads in time. Swing quavers, for example, lie somewhere between crotchet/quaver triplets and a dotted quaver/ semiquaver grouping.

Common time: $\frac{4}{4}$ time.

Chord I: The three-note chord built by adding a 3rd and a 5th above the first note of a scale. Other chords are similarly labelled: for example, Chord V is the chord built on the fifth note of the scale.

up-tempo numbers of the 1940s big band era. There had even been 'classical' composers using ragtime and the blues in their works, for example in George Gershwin's *Rhapsody in Blue* (1924).

THE BLUES STYLE

The country music equivalent for African Americans was the original folk blues of the Mississippi delta. This style was born towards the end of the 19th century and derives from a combination of the black field workers' improvisations and the ballads of that time. It is characterised by a heartfelt vocal delivery with lyrics often dealing with the realities of working life.

In the blues a regular beat in **common time** was provided by a guitar (and perhaps also, in the early years, by a washboard played as percussion). Often the guitar or harmonica was used to echo a vocal phrase, and singers delivered the repeated rhythms associated with the Mississippi delta with a rasp in their voice.

The melody would be built from the notes of a scale where the 3rd and the 7th notes were flattened (lowered by a semitone). This flattened 3rd would clash with the unflattened 3rd of **chord I**, and the flattened 7th, with the unflattened 7th of chord V creating a mournful or exhilarating sound depending on the tempo.

The sixth note was also sometimes flattened, creating more clashes. These notes became known as 'blue' notes, and the singer would often arrive at them by bending a note 'out of tune' in a very expressive way.

Many songs were constructed using a series of chords lasting for 12 bars:

I	I	I	I	IV	IV	I	I	V	V	I	I
IN KEY C MAJOR: | C | C | C | C | F | F | C | C | G | G | C | C |

There were several variations of this pattern. For example, chord IV was sometimes substituted for chord I in bar 2 and for chord V in bar 10. Also, chord V commonly replaced chord I on the last bar to help with the lead in to the next verse.

Rural blues musicians moved north to Memphis and further to Chicago and Detroit during the 1930s and 40s where factory work was available. In addition to greater employment prospects and increased wages these cities benefited from relatively well-equipped recording studios, offering greater opportunities for aspiring black artists.

Two important independent record labels were founded in 1950 in Memphis (Sun Records) and Chicago (Chess Records). The latter became the pre-eminent label for electric blues.

2

this book

Go to **www.hybridpublications.com** and enter the code **TR398**, which will unlock the supplementary resources for this book.

MUSICAL EXAMPLE

In the early years at Chess Records the blues artists adopted an amplified sound, with harmonica, slide guitar and piano as lead instruments. The composer, producer and bass player Willie Dixon was an important influence on the development of what became known as Chicago Blues. He worked with Muddy Waters, Howlin' Wolf and Little Walter, and later in the decade with Chuck Berry – all famous rhythm and bluesmen. Among his many compositions was the classic Muddy Waters song 'Hoochie Coochie Man'.

MUDDY WATERS, 'HOOCHIE COOCHIE MAN' (1954)

Written by Willie Dixon and recorded on the Chess label with
■ Muddy Waters – lead vocals and guitar
■ Little Walter – harmonica
■ Otis Spann – piano
■ Willie Dixon – bass
■ Fred Below - drums

The song begins in **stop time** using a short musical figure:

The figure is repeated with rests between while Waters sings the vocal line of the verse in a free and direct manner, following speech rhythms and a relatively restricted number of notes (mostly A and C). This affects the normal 12-bar structure because the first four bars are extended to eight. The silence is filled during the last repeat, which leads the music into:

0:25 the chord IV section, where Waters' vocal range extends to higher and more powerful notes. Here a full accompaniment is used with piano playing repeated **triplet** chords, harmonica interjecting with lead figures and tremolo shakes, and bass and drums supplying a heavy crotchet downbeat for the four-in-a-bar figure. The song has now become extended into a 16-bar structure.

0:55 During the last two bars of this, to serve as a lead-in to verse 2, the harmonies change every crotchet beat, ending on chord V⁷ (E⁷). A progression used in this way is known as a turnaround – a series of chords designed to lead either into the next section or back to the beginning of the last. The 16-bar structure is played three times through, and the guitar makes its presence felt more in the mix in verses 2 and 3 with a swung quaver **riff**.

02:41 The final verse ends with a favourite **cadence** formula with the bass moving upwards in crotchets – A, C♯, D, D♯, E . . . A.

The lyrics of the song refer to the Hoochie Coochie – a gypsy women's erotic dance performed at carnivals. The song is a classic of the time and has been covered by many great blues/R&B performers including Manfred Mann, Chuck Berry, Jimi Hendrix and Eric Clapton.

Muddy Waters

Stop time: Stop time is where a vocalist or solo instrumentalist performs bars unaccompanied, with the backing band punctuating the downbeats with short staccato chords.

Triplet: Three notes played in the time it normally takes for two.

Riff: A riff is a repeated ostinato figure used in song accompaniments. The term is more commonly used in pop and rock rather than classical music.

Cadence: Chords or implied harmonies that give the feeling of musical punctuation. A perfect cadence (chord V to chord I), for example, is the equivalent of a full stop.

3

Musical Examples

We have created playlists on Spotify and YouTube of all the Musical Examples featured in this book, so that you can access them with your preferred method.

Spotify   http://tinyURL.com/UPMSpotify
YouTube http://tinyURL.com/UPMyoutube
           Please note that Rhinegold
           Education is not responsible
           for the content of YouTube.

Track timings are provided to help the reader follow the analysis whilst listening to the audio.

Accompanying audio

The following audio examples are available on the website:

www.hybridpublications.com

Access code: TR398

About the author

David Ventura read music at Edinburgh University, has taught music in Scotland, Lancashire, Liverpool and the Isle of Wight, and was the director of music at Hereford Sixth Form College for fifteen years up until 2009. He has lectured nationwide on music technology and advised the UK Government on assessment in the National Curriculum for music at all key stages. He has acted as a consultant for the Qualifications and Curriculum Authority, was chair of the Southern Examining Group's GCSE panel, has examined for a number of boards, and has also run many teacher-training courses for Keynote Education. David has written a number of publications, including Rhinegold's *Film Music in Focus*, co-authoring the Rhinegold KS3 Elements series, and numerous articles for *Classroom Music* magazine. He is a prolific composer and enjoys playing jazz piano.

CHAPTER 1

The 1950s

BACKGROUND

During the 1950s there were a number of changes in US society. One of these was how white USA regarded the music of the African-American community and the consequences of this on the mainstream music industry. At the start of the decade black music – the folk blues of the Mississippi delta, the electric blues of Chicago, jazz, the gospel music of the churches and soul – was seen as separate to the music enjoyed by the middle-class white population. The ***Billboard*** pop charts of the early years of the decade included sweet country ballads, sentimental love songs and instrumental novelty numbers – for example, the 1952 hits 'I Saw Mommy Kissing Santa Claus' by Jimmy Boyd or the cowboy ballad 'High Noon – Do Not Forsake Me Oh My Darling' by Frankie Laine. The record companies that produced mainstream pop (Decca, Mercury, Columbia, Capitol and MGM) targeted the white US family, including their teenager children, and the music was wholesome and inoffensive. Network radio shows and the new medium of television broadcast the music of artists such as Perry Como, Frank Sinatra, Tony Bennett and Johnnie Ray. These artists' records dominated the charts on both sides of the Atlantic.

The chart lists published in *Billboard* were many and various. They included children's records, sheet music, jukebox plays, classical, England's top 20 and songs with the most TV performances. The three main categories, however, were pop, country and western, and rhythm & blues (R&B; listed as the 'Harlem Hit Parade' in earlier years). When a record appeared in more than one *Billboard* chart listing it was termed a **crossover**. White performers and their record companies would watch the R&B charts and identify songs doing well, then cover the songs, cleaning up the lyrics and making them hits in the pop charts, much to the annoyance of the original artists. These are not crossovers.

Syncopated and **swing** rhythms, blues and modal scales, improvisation and emotional directness – these are all examples of black musical techniques that had a profound effect on the development of US music. New Orleans jazz and the artistry of its black musicians had been incorporated into the music of white dance bands and featured prominently in the

Billboard Magazine was a magazine designed for the music industry and has been the definitive source for publishing record sales in the USA since the 1930s. It is very interesting to look at the back issues, available at **www.billboard.com/#/archive**. The UK had to wait until 1952 for the *New Musical Express* (NME) to publish its singles chart.

Crossover: This is applied to a record in the various US charts when it appears in more than one listing.

Syncopation: Syncopated music is accented in unusual places or has notes that are normally stressed missing. It became prominent in the days of piano ragtime composers such as Scott Joplin.

Swing: Music that swings has a bouncy character derived from subtle timing in the rhythms of notes against a regular beat. Listeners want to tap their feet or nod their heads in time. Swing quavers, for example, lie somewhere between crotchet/quaver triplets and a dotted quaver/semiquaver grouping.

Common time: $\frac{4}{4}$ time.

Chord I: The three-note chord built by adding a 3rd and a 5th above the first note of a scale. Other chords are similarly labelled: for example, chord V is the chord built on the fifth note of the scale.

up-tempo numbers of the 1940s big band era. There had even been 'classical' composers using ragtime and the blues in their works, for example in George Gershwin's *Rhapsody in Blue* (1924).

THE BLUES STYLE

The country music equivalent for African Americans was the original folk blues of the Mississippi delta. This style was born towards the end of the 19th century and derives from a combination of the black field workers' improvisations and the ballads of that time. It is characterised by a heartfelt vocal delivery with lyrics often dealing with the realities of working life.

In the blues a regular beat in **common time** was provided by a guitar (and perhaps also, in the early years, by a washboard played as percussion). Often the guitar or harmonica was used to echo a vocal phrase, and singers delivered the repeated rhythms associated with the Mississippi delta with a rasp in their voice.

The melody would be built from the notes of a scale where the 3rd and the 7th notes were flattened (lowered by a semitone). This flattened 3rd would clash with the unflattened 3rd of **chord I**, and the flattened 7th, with the unflattened 7th of chord V creating a mournful or exhilarating sound depending on the tempo.

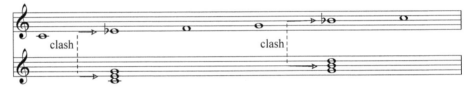

The sixth note was also sometimes flattened, creating more clashes. These notes became known as 'blue' notes, and the singer would often arrive at them by bending a note 'out of tune' in a very expressive way.

Many songs were constructed using a series of chords lasting for 12 bars:

There were several variations of this pattern. For example, chord IV was sometimes substituted for chord I in bar 2 and for chord V in bar 10. Also, chord V commonly replaced chord I on the last bar to help with the lead in to the next verse.

Rural blues musicians moved north to Memphis and further to Chicago and Detroit during the 1930s and 40s where factory work was available. In addition to greater employment prospects and increased wages for workers, these cities benefited from relatively well-equipped recording studios, offering greater opportunities for aspiring black artists.

Two important independent record labels were founded in 1950 in Memphis (Sun Records) and Chicago (Chess Records). The latter became the pre-eminent label for electric blues.

In the early years at Chess Records the blues artists adopted an amplified sound, with harmonica, slide guitar and piano as lead instruments. The composer, producer and bass player Willie Dixon was an important influence on the development of what became known as Chicago Blues. He worked with Muddy Waters, Howlin' Wolf and Little Walter, and later in the decade with Chuck Berry – all famous rhythm and bluesmen. Among his many compositions was the classic Muddy Waters song 'Hoochie Coochie Man'.

MUSICAL EXAMPLE

MUDDY WATERS, 'HOOCHIE COOCHIE MAN' (1954)

Written by Willie Dixon and recorded on the Chess label with

- Muddy Waters – lead vocals and guitar
- Little Walter – harmonica
- Otis Spann – piano
- Willie Dixon – bass
- Fred Below - drums

Muddy Waters

The song begins in **stop time** using a short musical figure:

The figure is repeated with rests between while Waters sings the vocal line of the verse in a free and direct manner, following speech rhythms and a relatively restricted number of notes (mostly A and C). This affects the normal 12-bar structure because the first four bars are extended to eight. The silence is filled during the last repeat, which leads the music into:

0:35 the chord IV section, where Waters' vocal range extends to higher and more powerful notes. Here a full accompaniment is used with piano playing repeated **triplet** chords, harmonica interjecting with lead figures and tremolo shakes, and bass and drums supplying a heavy crotchet downbeat for the four-in-a-bar figure. The song has now become extended into a 16-bar structure.

0:55 During the last two bars of this, to serve as a lead-in to verse 2, the harmonies change every crotchet beat, ending on chord V⁷ (E⁷). A progression used in this way is known as a turnaround – a series of chords designed to lead either into the next section or back to the beginning of the last. The 16-bar structure is played three times through, and the guitar makes its presence felt more in the mix in verses 2 and 3 with a swung quaver **riff**.

02:41 The final verse ends with a favourite **cadence** formula with the bass moving upwards in crotchets – A, C♯, D, D♯, E … A.

The lyrics of the song refer to the Hoochie Coochie – a gypsy women's erotic dance performed at carnivals. The song is a classic of the time and has been covered by many great blues/R&B performers including Manfred Mann, Chuck Berry, Jimi Hendrix and Eric Clapton.

Stop time: Stop time is where a vocalist or solo instrumentalist performs bars unaccompanied, with the backing band punctuating the downbeats with short staccato chords.

Triplet: Three notes played in the time it normally takes for two.

Riff: A riff is a repeated ostinato figure used in song accompaniments. The term is more commonly used in pop and rock rather than classical music.

Cadence: Chords or implied harmonies that give the feeling of musical punctuation. A perfect cadence (chord V to chord I), for example, is the equivalent of a full stop.

3

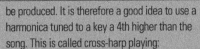

MUSICAL INSTRUMENT

THE HARMONICA

This is also known as the mouth organ, and in pop as the blues harp. Little Walter was famous for his ability on the harmonica and produced a hit demonstrating his solo skills in 1952, called 'Juke'. The harmonica was a favourite instrument of blues performers as they liked its expressive qualities and its ability to bend notes much the same as the guitar was able to do. It could also be attached to a neck rack, which enabled solo performers to play guitar at the same time as using the harmonica to play lead **phrases** both between the vocal phrases and for an instrumental verse. Harmonicas are normally tuned to one key (diatonic). The common ten-hole version will produce the notes of chord I when blown and the other notes of the scale when drawn (sucked). Notes can be overblown (or overdrawn) to bend the pitch, and, when more drawing than blowing is used, notes of the blues scale can

be produced. It is therefore a good idea to use a harmonica tuned to a key a 4th higher than the song. This is called cross-harp playing:

- To play blues in G you need a harmonica in C
- To play blues in E you need a harmonica in A
- To play blues in A you need a harmonica in D
- To play blues in C you need a harmonica in F
- To play blues in D you need a harmonica in G

The holes of a C harmonica produce the following notes:

Notes of a harmonica

Phrase: A subdivision of a tune. For example, tunes are often made up of four-bar phrases.

Harmonica players would use a range of techniques to produce variation in tone:

Tone variation	Description	Technique
Pitch bend	Tuning of note slides up or down	Overblowing or overdrawing
Vibrato	Regular variation in pitch	Adjusting embouchure (facial muscles)
Tremolo	Movement between two notes adjacent on the instrument (such as between C and E)	Head shaking
Sound-level tremolo	Regular variation in dynamic (loud and soft)	Cupping the hands and the instrument and rapidly opening and closing them
Power sound	Little Walter's technique	Enclosing a microphone and harmonica together in the hands

RHYTHM AND BLUES

This genre derives from a combination of jazz and rural blues, but it is not a single musical style. Rather, it is a term that covers all music played by black musicians intended for black urban listeners. It remained separate from mainstream pop, and country and western during the years 1945–55, with no one expecting white listeners to buy the records or listen to the regional radio stations that were dedicated to the genre.

The table on the next page lists some of the R&B hits from the first five years of the decade. African-American artists performed all the examples, although some white songwriters were involved. It is not meant to be comprehensive, simply a selection of the great songs that are worth listening to.

RECOMMENDED LISTENING

Released	Single	Artist
1950	'Cupid Boogie'	Little Esther Phillips
	'Blue Light Boogie'	Louis Jordan
	'The Fat Man'	Fats Domino
	'Teardrops From My Eyes'	Ruth Brown
1951	'Three O'Clock In The Morning'	B.B. King
	'Bad, Bad Whisky'	Amos Milburn
	'Rocket 88'	Jackie Brenston and his Delta Cats
	'I Got Loaded'	Peppermint Harris
1952	'Hound Dog'	Big Mama Thornton
	'5-10-15 Hours'	Ruth Brown
	'Have Mercy Baby'	The Dominoes
	'Booted'	Roscoe Gordon
1953	'Honey Hush'	Big Joe Turner
	'Mess Around'	Ray Charles
	'Money Honey'	Clyde McPhatter and The Drifters
	'Baby Don't Do It'	The 5 Royales
1954	'I Got A Woman'	Ray Charles
	'Sh-Boom'	The Chords
	'The Things That I Used To Do'	Guitar Slim
	'Work With Me Annie'	Hank Ballard and the Midnighters

Many of these tracks use a swing or shuffle rhythm. Found extensively in jazz, the style employs a walking bass (continuous crotchets moving in scale or **arpeggio** patterns), and melodies and drums featuring swung quavers:

> **Arpeggio:** Notes from a chord played one after another.

The boogie (or boogie woogie) was a up-tempo piano shuffle featuring a repeated pattern in the left hand, such as:

Piano boogie was a speciality of the popular R&B crossover artist Fats Domino, who had hits throughout the decade (such as 'Ain't That A Shame', 1955, or 'Blueberry Hill', 1956).

Louis Jordan and His Tympany Five

Rhythm section: This was
the section of a group that
kept things going, providing
the harmonic and rhythmic
framework for the rest of the
band. It comprised piano,
guitar, bass and drums.

JUMP BLUES

One of the most exciting artists of the late 1940s and early 1950s was Louis Jordan,
accompanied by His Tympany Five, with tracks such as 'Blue Light Boogie'. His style could
be seen as a precursor to rock and roll, and it is interesting to note that he had a number
of hits in the pop listings. He spearheaded the 1940s style known as 'jump blues', and
slimmed down the traditional big-band line-up of five saxes and eight brass, to a small
combo of just a **rhythm section** with his own saxophone. The music was made for
dancing, with its strong beat and fast tempi, and as it became more popular it added a
strong vocalist to the line-up. Jordan was a consummate entertainer with an engaging
personality. His vocals employed humorous lyrics but sometimes would refer to social
issues such as racism or poverty.

THE GOSPEL STYLE

Gospel music, as its name suggests, comes from the church, where in the early years of the
20th-century black attendees combined their work songs and hymns into negro spirituals
such as 'Swing Low, Sweet Chariot'. Many of the workers who attended these churches
were unable to read, but to involve them in the proceedings they were asked to repeat
the words of the preacher – creating music with a 'call-and-response' phrasing. Ad lib
handclapping and vocalisations were common, and when a rhythm and a pulse were added
gospel music was born. Later, instruments were added – such as piano, organ, guitar and
tambourine – and faster tempi were adopted. The black radio presenter Joe Bostic helped
to popularise gospel music on his shows, and as a concert promoter was responsible for
producing the Negro Gospel and Religious Music Festival at Carnegie Hall in 1950. When
this style of music adopted secular lyrics and moved away from the church, it became
known as soul.

Other influential soul singers from the 1950s include the flamboyant James Brown
('Please, Please, Please', 1956) and Sam Cooke (a lyrical contrast to James Brown,
producing more soulful ballads).

MUSICAL EXAMPLE

RAY CHARLES, 'WHAT'D I SAY' (1959)

Ray Charles fused R&B, gospel and blues styles into something new – soul music. The major hits of his early career include 'Mess Around' (1953), a barrel-house heavy boogie woogie, 'I Got A Woman' (1954), an up-tempo jump swing, and 'Drown In My Own Tears' (1956), a $^{12}_8$ ballad. 'What'd I Say' was in **straight eights** and therefore closer to modern rock: a soul crossover record and popular with both black and white audiences.

Ray Charles

Straight eights: A $^4_4$ rhythm where the quavers are mostly even.

Solo break: A short passage where a soloist continues on his or her own while the rest of the band stop.

Acciaccaturas: Sometimes known as crushed notes, they are very fast notes that immediately precede the main one, sounding as if they have been crushed into it.

Horns: In pop and jazz the term refers to trumpets, trombones and saxes, not French horns as in classical music.

The song begins with Charles playing a repeated two-bar riff on a Wurlitzer electric piano that is transposed according to the 12-bar-blues harmonic structure:

The quavers in Charles' 12-bar solo introduction sometimes drift towards swing quavers, but when the rhythm section comes in there is no doubt that the song is in straight eights.

0:16　He plays a right-hand piano riff over the top of the music quoted above and finishes the 12 bars with a extra little fancy fill.

0:31　This heralds four bars of piano **solo breaks** with the rhythm section simply punching out the first beats of the bar in stop time. He uses **acciaccaturas** (shown as the small 'crossed out' notes) to try to dig between the keys of the piano. Piano players were unable to bend notes like harmonica players could and reverted to these tricks to emulate the bluesmen.

The solo breaks, with their wide variety of inventiveness demonstrating Ray Charles' keyboard ability, are used again and again for the first four bars of the 12-bar sequence until at 1:36 finally the vocals enter with:

> Hey mama, don't you treat me wrong
> Come and love your daddy all night long
> All right now, hey hey, all right.

The first two lines of this section are treated as stops and the third line is used to complete the 12 bars, just the as in the instrumental sections previously.

2:41　After four vocal verses he returns to instrumental then back to vocals again.

3:45　Eventually he reaches a kind of chorus to the words of the title, which introduces a fuller accompaniment with **horns** playing rhythmic chords in the background.

4:17　Suddenly everything stops and the music is replaced with speech as if at a party.

4:30　Ray Charles launches into a call-and-response section as he sings 'Hey' and the partygoers reply with 'Ho'.

- This repeats until the chorus returns to the words 'Say it one more time'.
- More choruses and call-and-response sections follow, giving the concluding section of the song a genuine improvised character.

A Wurlitzer electric piano

MUSICAL INSTRUMENT

THE ELECTRIC PIANO

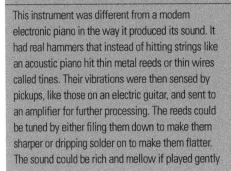

This instrument was different from a modern electronic piano in the way it produced its sound. It had real hammers that instead of hitting strings like an acoustic piano hit thin metal reeds or thin wires called tines. Their vibrations were then sensed by pickups, like those on an electric guitar, and sent to an amplifier for further processing. The reeds could be tuned by either filing them down to make them sharper or dripping solder on to make them flatter. The sound could be rich and mellow if played gently or more cutting and metallic when played with force. The most famous makes were the Wurlitzer (used on the track on the previous page by Ray Charles) which notably opens the Supertramp track 'Dreamer' from the album *Crime of the Century* (1974) with repeated chords, the Fender Rhodes, which was a particular favourite of jazzmen, and the Hohner Pianet. Yamaha, Baldwin and Kawai electric pianos actually amplified wire strings and sounded more like an acoustic piano.

DOO-WOP

Many young black performers couldn't afford musical instruments and got together to form singing groups, combining the harmonies and techniques of white singing groups (such as the barbershop-style Mills Brothers and the Andrews Sisters) with gospel music from their church. The term doo-wop derives from the nonsense syllables often included in the backing or sometimes in the main lyrics. The words were an attempt to imitate instruments:

- doo-wop or doo-wah = brass instruments sounds using wah-wah mutes
- shang-a-lang = twangy rhythm guitar
- bom-bom-bom = bass guitar
- doomph, doomph = an acoustic bass.

The normal texture would feature a lead vocal part with three or four backing singers.

Initially they performed in the streets, some even taking part in singing competitions between rival groups, but later were taken into studios where the resident musicians would listen to the music and then create an accompaniment to go with it. Groups from the late 1940s and early 1950s tended to be named after birds, such as The Swallows, The Ravens, The Orioles, The Penguins, The Crows, The Flamingos and The Larks. Famous bands include The Platters with their hits 'Only You' and 'The Great Pretender' (both 1955) and Frankie Lymon and The Teenagers with 'Why Do Fools Fall In Love' (1956).

Doo-wop as a sub-genre died a natural death with the advent of rock and roll, but its influence can be traced in the music of The Four Seasons and The Beach Boys (see Chapter 2)

MUSICAL EXAMPLE

THE CHORDS, 'SH-BOOM' (1954)

The band was spotted in a subway. Its five members were:

- Carl Feaster (lead vocals)
- Claude Feaster (baritone)
- James 'Jimmy' Keyes (first tenor)
- Floyd 'Buddy' McRae (second tenor)
- James 'Ricky' Edwards (bass)

Male voices divide into tenor (high), baritone (medium) and bass (low).

The Chords

A huge hit in both the R&B charts (number 3) and the pop charts (number 9), 'Sh-Boom' was released by Atlantic Records, an independent company that tried to reach a wide audience and specialised in black pop.

0:00 It begins with a four-bar intro, the singers performing in block harmony:

- two bars **a cappella**
- two bars with a rhythm section of guitar, acoustic plucked bass and drums played with wire brushes.

0:07 The main song then starts with Carl singing the lead lyrics while the others sing oo, wah and sh-boom in the background. For the first eight bars the harmonies follow a formula very common with doo-wop groups (chords I I VI I IV or II I V II) – so common that it has become known as the 50s progression. In this case F I Dm I Gm I C II is the progression.

0:21 There then follows a four-bar interlude over the same chords with the lead singing even more nonsense syllables.

0:28 The eight bars from the main song are repeated.

0:43 The music then moves to a contrasting middle section with Ricky Edwards singing a rich lead bass line over the chords A^7 I A^7 I D^7 I D^7 I G^7 I G^7 I Gm I C^7 I sung by the others. The harmonies in this section form another well-used progression known as a **cycle of 5ths**. The last two bars form a turnaround back to:

0:57 a repeat of the opening progression but this time in full close harmony, making the structure AABA (plus the four-bar interlude): a common pop music formula. However, the eight bars are now repeated with the first four bars using the nonsense material from the interlude and the last four from the intro (let's call this C).

1:21 Next, there is a 16-bar instrumental tenor sax solo in a laid-back jazz style that leads back to:

1:52 an eight-bar closing section the same as C and closing with a jazzy sounding F major 7th chord:

A cappella: Vocal music performed without accompaniment. The term comes from the Italian for 'in church', where singing would be normally without instruments in early music.

Cycle of 5ths: A harmonic pattern where each chord has a root note a 5th lower than the last: A I D I G I C, and so on.

ROCK AND ROLL

Another fundamental change to pop music during the 1950s was the rise of a teenage culture, independent from adults and the family. Young people would seek out music that had a more exciting edge. It was black music, R&B, that they began to listen to, on records and on the radio, especially the newly invented portable transistor radios and the AM radios in cars. The teenager became the most important purchaser of records, forcing record companies to take previously marginalised styles more seriously.

The white-owned record companies recognised a potential market concentrating on the new purchasing power of the now slightly more affluent black listeners from the cities. However, it took the formation of a small independent record label named Sun Records in 1950 to really move things forward. Sam Phillips, the owner, wanted to bring black music to white audiences and loved the R&B style. Phillips recorded artists such as B.B. King and Howlin' Wolf, but in 1953 a young country boy named Elvis walked into the studio.

Elvis Presley was exactly what Phillips was looking for – a white singer who could put across his songs with the energy and vocal tones used by black performers. He recorded the sad ballad 'That's All Right' transforming it into an energetic rock and roll number. Later Elvis signed up with RCA records and was to become one of the great icons of 20th-century pop with songs such as 'Hound Dog' (1956), 'All Shook Up' (1957), 'Blue Suede Shoes' (1956) and 'Jailhouse Rock' (1957) – definitive rock and roll numbers.

In 1951 a white teenage band with Bill Haley as the lead vocalist recorded a cover version of Jackie Brenston and his Delta Cats' 'Rocket 88' – which sang the praises of a new car. It was produced just a few months after the original had reached the top of the R&B charts. His country group gave the song a totally new style, and music historians often quote it as the first rock and roll song. In 1953 Bill Haley and His Comets recorded 'Crazy Man, Crazy' which was used as the soundtrack for a play starring James Dean, and consequently became was the first rock and roll song to be broadcast on television. It wasn't until 1954 that Haley and his band produced 'Rock Around The Clock'. This was made famous the following year when it appeared as the soundtrack to the film *Blackboard Jungle*, a feature of which was teenage rebellion.

Bill Haley and His Comets

The rock and roll style had its eye to the pop charts, utilising an exciting youthful dynamism that caught the imagination of teenagers across the world. It was a fusion of several different genres:

R&B made from jazz combined with rural blues, using a swing beat and notes of the blues scale **+** Country music with the acoustic foot-tapping up-tempo character of Appalachian folk music, bluegrass and hillbilly styles **+** Gospel-influenced heartfelt vocal expression **=** Rock and roll

The early songs of the genre recorded by country bands are described as rockabilly, but black artists such as Little Richard also recorded rock and roll. Some other famous rock and roll or rockabilly songs of the decade are listed below:

Released	Single	Artist
1954	'Shake, Rattle and Roll'	Bill Haley and His Comets, cover version of Big Joe Turner original – with 'cleaned up' lyrics
1955	'Tutti Frutti'	Little Richard
	'Blue Suede Shoes'	Carl Perkins
	'Maybelline'	Chuck Berry
1956	'Long Tall Sally'	Little Richard
	'Be-Bop-A-Lula'	Gene Vincent
1957	'Lucille'	Little Richard
	'Whole Lot Of Shakin' Going On'	Jerry Lee Lewis
	'Great Balls Of Fire'	Jerry Lee Lewis
	'Peggy Sue'	Buddy Holly
	'Oh Boy'	Buddy Holly
1958	'Good Golly Miss Molly'	Little Richard
	'Sweet Little Sixteen'	Chuck Berry
	'Johnny B. Goode'	Chuck Berry
	'Rave On'	Buddy Holly
	'Summertime Blues'	Eddie Cochran
	'Move It'	Cliff Richard
1959	'Memphis Tennessee'	Chuck Berry

1959 was the year that *Billboard Magazine* combined all its various charts into one and called it The Hot 100.

Walking bass: Bass notes that move with a constant common duration, usually crotchets. Often walking bass lines are made from combining scales and arpeggios.

Open string: Notes that use open strings are not created by pressing down with the fingers on a fret or fingerboard, but just plucked, strummed or bowed producing the natural note of the string. They have more resonance than stopped notes.

MUSICAL EXAMPLE

CARL PERKINS, 'BLUE SUEDE SHOES' (1955)

Carl Perkins

Perkins grew up as a poor fieldworker in Tennessee. He was heavily influenced by Nashville's country and western styles, and performed with his brothers in bars and on local radio. But when he heard Bill Monroe's classic country waltz 'Blue Moon Of Kentucky' broadcast on the radio in an up-tempo rockabilly version by Elvis Presley he decided to go to Sun Studios, where Elvis first started his recording career. He was in luck and was able to make several recordings and tour extensively as a support act for Elvis himself. He became known as the 'King of Rockabilly'.

In the stop time at the start of the song, Perkins adds two extra beats at the ends of the first two bars, building anticipation as he runs through his one, two, three list of arriving at a dance hall.

The rhythm section then picks up the beat with a **walking bass** from a double bass, acoustic rhythm guitar, drums and Perkins playing electric guitar.

0:18   More stop time follows as this time Perkins lists the dos and don'ts of behaviour near his favourite shoes.

0:41   An instrumental chorus follows where he demonstrates his ability as a lead electric guitar with repeated blue notes sliding into tune, sometimes creating a clash with its next-door **open string**, combined with syncopated rhythmic chords.

0:57   The song format then repeats leading to

1:20   a second guitar solo and finishes with a third play-through, and then

1:53   a 12-bar chorus to the words of the title rounds things off.

It is interesting to compare the stage versions of Elvis Presley's cover of 'Blue Suede Shoes', released slightly later in 1956, with the Carl Perkins original. The versions use exactly the same line-up, and although both performers enjoy dancing about during the guitar instrumental, Presley delegates the lead guitar to another member of the band. This allows him to gyrate more energetically, playing to his audience.

Rockabilly was an early form of rock and roll that drew on country roots, and the early recordings of Elvis Presley and Buddy Holly were in this style. Buddy Holly moved away from rockabilly as his career developed. He was a talented songwriter and had an enormous influence on the music of the 1960s, particularly in Britain. His tragic death in a plane crash in 1959 is seen by some as the end of rock and roll.

BUDDY HOLLY, 'PEGGY SUE' (1957)

This song shows Holly's originality as a songwriter. He uses a minimal line-up of drums and double bass, accompanying himself on electric guitar, the combination being employed very economically but yet producing a highly exciting and memorable composition.

Buddy Holly

The music gets under way with a four-bar intro using the chords A | D | A | E :|| During this the drums play a pounding semiquaver rhythm using only the tom toms in the drum kit, pre-empting The Surfaris' hit 'Wipe Out' by five years.

The main verse uses a 12-bar structure but is not in a blues idiom.

0:25   A second verse follows leading to:

0:45   a third 12-bar sequence, this time notable for the unusual inclusion of a ♭VI chord (F major in the key of A), emphasising the name of the girl in the song title.

1:04   Then comes a fourth verse in the same format, but interest is maintained through the use of the fast tempo, driving drums and Holly's unique vocal tones.

1:24   An instrumental follows, again over the 12 bars, featuring Holly's electric guitar playing fast rhythmic chords low on the instrument and on open strings, giving away his country origins.

1:44   The next two vocal verses suddenly drop the volume low – another innovative touch for a rock and roll song. The tom tom drums are faded in and out between the vocals.

2:23   The song finishes with a four-bar tag.

Other major hits of Buddy Holly and The Crickets include:

| 1957 | 'That'll Be The Day'; 'Oh Boy!' | 1959 | 'It Doesn't Matter Anymore' (posthumous) |
| 1958 | 'Rave On'; 'Heartbeat' | 1960 | 'True Love Ways' (posthumous) |

THE DRUM KIT

The components of the drum kit were standardised in the 1930s and remained more or less constant until the excesses of the 1960s expanded them. They consisted of:

- Bass drum with pedal – also known as a kick drum.
- Snare drum – snares are twisted metal wires under the drum that vibrate against the head (skin). A lever was attached that would lift them away from the surface of the drum head so that a less rattling sound could be obtained.
- Floor and mounted tom toms – drums that sound deeper than the snare.
- High hat – small cymbals played by combining foot pedal and stick.
- Larger cymbals – ride cymbals (used for continuous rhythms) and the slightly smaller crash cymbal (used for emphasis at important moments). Some larger ride cymbals (known as sizzle cymbals) would have holes drilled into them with inserted rivets that would create a more continuous wash of sound.

The sound the drums produced could be varied either by using different kinds of beaters – heavy or light sticks (heavy for rock, light for jazz), wire brushes or felt-ended timpani sticks for a less sharp sound. Also, the drum heads could be played in different places – for example, in the centre for a full sound, near the edge for a bright sound and on the rim for a click.

Ever since the 1920s drums were essential in providing a constant rhythmic background in up-tempo pop music. In the 1940s they were part of a big band's rhythm section until virtuosi such as Gene Krupa and Buddy Rich featured them as solo instruments. In some circumstances they were replaced by cheaper alternatives – in the UK a country/jazz style called skiffle developed which used a washboard to provide the rhythmic element (along with a string stretched between a tea chest and a broom handle for a bass). In the 1970s electronic drums were introduced.

Reproduced with kind permission of www.start-drumming.com

No chapter on pop music of the 1950s is complete without a look at one of the recordings of Elvis Presley.

Family watching TV in the 1950s. Although the television was invented in the 1920s, its mass manufacture was prevented by World War Two. Regular network television broadcasts began in the USA in 1948, although the BBC had been transmitting in the UK since 1936.

MUSICAL EXAMPLE

ELVIS PRESLEY, 'HOUND DOG' (1956)

Unlike Buddy Holly, Presley was not a songwriter. He had songs written for him by establishment composers and he covered many other bands' earlier hits, often making them much more famous than the originals.

'Hound Dog' was written by Jerry Leiber and Mike Stoller for Big Mama Thornton in 1952 and was a heavy R&B rock number. Elvis recorded the song shortly after he was signed by RCA and transformed it into up-tempo white rock and roll. His good looks and stage presence made him a very visual performer. When he appeared on television on the Milton Berle Show to sing the song, he abandoned his guitar so that he could more effectively communicate with his audience via physical dance movements, and the shots of enthusiastic young girls in the audience helped to create a live atmosphere for the viewers. He followed this appearance with several more TV shows in quick succession, and the national exposure was an important step-up for his career. This song was an ideal vehicle to cement his growing status as a teenage idol.

- Elvis fires straight in with a lead vocal break – no intro, no beating about the bush, just a direct holler on the blue flattened 3rd of the scale (E♭ in C major).

- The first verse starts, following the 12-bar blues sequence, with a bass line derived from rising triads (the basic three-note chord) to the regular rhythm and concluding with a fierce triplet break on the snare (a moment for Elvis to waggle on the TV show).

0:16 Verse 2 is a copy of verse 1 with 'High class' lyrics.

0:33 Verse 3 is a copy of verse 1 with 'Hound dog'.

0:49 Guitar solo verse with vocal backing singing sustained chords.

1:05 Verse 4 is the same as verse 2.

1:22 A second guitar solo, again with vocal backing.

1:37 Verse 5 is the same as verse 2.

1:54 Verse 6 is the same as verse 1, ending with the last line of the lyrics unaccompanied, followed by a short cadence.

This simple verse form is very direct and uncomplicated, its main focus being on driving the music forwards. It was also easy for fans to learn and sing themselves.

POP MUSIC IN THE UK

In the early years of the 1950s US artists such as Frank Sinatra and Doris Day dominated the British charts, with the exception of the wartime favourite Vera Lynn. If there were successful home-produced artists then they would cover US hits (for example, Jimmy Young with his 'Unchained Melody', written by the film composer Alex North). However, in 1954–55 a new type of music that combined country and western styles with jazz was born, and became a uniquely British phenomenon called skiffle. Its leading exponent was the guitar vocalist Lonnie Donnegan, who had a string of number-one hits including 'Cumberland Gap' and 'Puttin' On The Style' (both 1957). The genre faded out in the early 1960s but partly because of its use of homemade instruments (such as washboard and tea-chest bass) it left an important legacy of amateurism, which was crucial in developing the youth music-making culture that was to follow.

Young people in the UK spent much of their time listening to US records, especially rock and roll. This music was adopted by the teddy boys, a fashion-conscious set of young people seen as juvenile delinquents and a cultural threat to society at the time. In 1958 Britain's answer to Elvis, the singer Cliff Richard and his band The Drifters (later to become The Shadows – a group that recorded instrumental hits in their own right), recorded 'Move It'. The song was performed on ITV's teenage music show 'Oh Boy!' and is often cited as the UK's first real rock and roll recording.

MUSICAL EXAMPLE

CLIFF RICHARD, 'MOVE IT' (1958)

Cliff Richard

Licks: Short stock musical phrases (not repeated like riffs).

0:00 — An exciting lead electric guitar break tumbles down and settles on playing regular repeated quavers as a solid backing. It uses the open 5ths of E and B on the lowest two strings of the guitar, and sets the driving tempo of the music.

0:17 — After six bars of rhythm the vocals enter with a sound processed by tape echo in the style of Elvis' early recordings, with two-bar phrases answered by a second electric guitar filling in with high, wailing **licks**. This repeats, making a total of 16 bars (with the last phrase referring to rock and roll directly in the lyrics).

0:41 — The harmony moves to chord IV and follows the blues sequence of chords leading to:

1:04 — a guitar instrumental section followed by:

1:29 — a repeat of the song.

The chord progression of the song after the intro is therefore: 16 bars of E; 4 bars of A; 4 bars of E; 2 bars of B; 2 bars of A; 4 bars of E.

The song is notable on three counts:

1. The constant driving quavers from the guitar, keeping things going as the bass and drums drop out. When they re-enter they are used to build up the sense of forward motion. This technique illustrates the lyrics that include words such as 'move it' and 'drives along' – even being unable to stop at the end, but gradually fading out, as if heading off into the distance.
2. Its very electric sound, less countrified than some rock and roll.
3. Its constant use of blue notes, not in an expressive sliding blues style but as notes of a scale or mode in their own right.

This foreshadowed the beat music that was to dominate pop music in both the UK and the USA in the next decade.

DEVELOPMENTS IN MUSIC TECHNOLOGY

- In 1948 vinyl records, both the 12-inch 33^1/$_3$ rpm long play (LP) and the 7-inch 45 rpm single began to be produced. Singles (45s) went on to sell much more than everyone expected, their 3-minute format suiting teenagers' tastes. The vinyl record jukebox was introduced in 1950.

- The microphone had been an important technological development of earlier years: its introduction meant that singers no longer had to project their voices above the sound of a band and could perform in a more intimate way, as with the early 'crooners' such as Bing Crosby. The common choice of 1950s stage work was the Shure 55S dynamic microphone, able to avoid speaker feedback by having a good **unidirectional** response. Also **bi-directional** ribbon microphones were in common use, particularly for backing singers.

- In 1954 Leo Fender introduced the Fender Stratocaster guitar – an electric guitar that became a classic. It featured a solid body with three-single coil pickups and was much sleeker than its earlier cousin from 1949 – the Fender Telecaster. Electric guitar technology had been developed by the Gibson company, and before the Fender series these were semi-acoustic models (see p 25).

- In 1955 the Hammond B3 electric organ was introduced. This was to become a favourite instrument in the late 1950s and through the 1960s with its revolutionary way of producing sound through additive synthesis. This featured a row of drawbars that were tuned to different notes of the harmonic series and could be combined together (see p 33).

- In 1957 the German company EMT (Elektromesstecknik) released the EMT 140 Plate Reverberation Unit. Plate reverb used a suspended metal sheet that vibrated in response to the sound, and the result was a bright reverberation that became the standard in studios during the 1960s and 70s.

- In 1958 Charlie Watkins invented the WEM Copicat, a sound-processing unit based on magnetic tape loops that passed a recording head, several playback heads and an erase head, in that order, in a neat portable unit. The result was that echoes or delays were added to the audio signal. Bands used them on vocals and lead guitar parts. Tape echo had been used in studios (particularly at Sun Studios, where Elvis Presley's processed vocals became a trademark sound) but this involved multiple tape players or a process of feeding back the output signal from the playback head of a tape recorder to its record head. The convenient WEM Copicat became a worldwide best-selling piece of equipment.

Unidirectional: Coming from one direction.
Bi-directional: Coming from two directions. Bi-directional microphones pick up well from either side, making them ideal for two singers facing each other. They used a thin ribbon of aluminium between the poles of a magnet, but this sometimes caused problems because of its fragility.

CHAPTER 2

The 1960s (part 1)

BACKGROUND

The 1960s was a decade of social upheaval. Teenage culture increased its influence on daily life and older people felt the very fabric of society was being challenged. The feminist movement became more powerful and the general public became aware of environmental issues. In Britain the Campaign for Nuclear Disarmament became a mass movement, and in the USA the population expressed it ideas through the Civil Rights Movement and the protests against the Vietnam War. Here the WSP (Women Strike for Peace) gathered 50,000 women to demonstrate against national policy. Folk musicians regularly produced protest songs to galvanise public opinion, exemplified by Joan Baez ('What Have They Done To The Rain', 1962) and Bob Dylan ('Blowin' In The Wind', 1963). The assassination of President John F. Kennedy in 1963 turned a nation full of optimism into one with an increasingly cynical view of life.

In the UK, the rationing of wartime that had lasted into the 1950s was a thing of the past, and working-class people now had real spending power. Harold Macmillan, the Prime Minister in the UK from 1957 to 1963, said that the British people had 'never had it so good', and London became the fashion capital of the world. Immigration became a difficult issue as black and Asian families came to Britain from the Commonwealth. The phrase 'the permissive society' became associated with young people.

In the late 1950s, during the first wave of rock and roll, there had been a rise in independent record labels, and artists had gained control of the composition and production of their music. At the start of the 1960s, however, the pop charts in the USA became dominated by large corporations, and a partial return to the way business was done before 1955 took place. This was the safe option, with the unpredictable and challenging music of R&B being brought under the control of the experienced music-industry professionals. The Brill Building in Manhattan, New York, housed many of the offices and studios where pop songs were written. Here would be found teams of composers and lyricists, arrangers and session musicians churning out pop songs in the same way as the old **Tin Pan Alley** writers had done. It was a veritable production line.

Tin Pan Alley: This was the name given to an area of Manhattan where music publishers and songwriters produced much of the music to dominate the popular music of the USA in the first half of the 20th century. Its importance eventually died out at the start of the rock and roll years.

The Brill Building, New York

Mono: Short for monophonic. Recording on a single track, so the sound is identical in both speakers if played on stereo equipment.

The Aldon Music Publishing Company was housed near the Brill Building at 1650 Broadway. On its books were singer-songwriters such as Carole King and Neil Sedaka, two performers that bucked the trend as they were able to perform their own work. However, they had to work as a team with a lyricist – Carole King with Gerry Goffin, and Neil Sedaka with Howard Greenfield – producing a song every few days. When a record company acquired a song it would engage an A&R (artists and repertoire) representative, whose job it was to organise the recording session, first producing a **mono** backing track with the house musicians before considering the lead vocalists. There would often be large numbers involved, with orchestral accompaniments and groups of backing singers, plus technicians.

The record companies targeted young people, and this resulted in a brand of manufactured pop music that focused on producing a teen idol – sometimes a handsome young man whose musical talents might not be top rate. Neil Sedaka's musical talents, however, do not come into question.

Other famous teen idols of the time included Paul Anka and Bobby Darin, who also wrote their own songs. Many would appear on the popular TV show *American Bandstand*, which often gave them instant success. There was a studio audience of adoring teenagers, but to take no chances the show's producers would expect performers to mime to their recordings rather than sing live. Dancing was encouraged, and in 1960 the show's presenter Dick Clark introduced Chubby Checker and his version of 'The Twist'. Other dances followed, including the fly, the fish and the mashed potato. Little Eva's famous dance 'The Loco-Motion' that did so well in the charts (number 1 in the USA, number 2 in the UK) was featured on ABC's variety show series *Shindig* in 1964.

Along with the teenager pop idol there was another trend affecting the US pop charts of the time. Folk music had become increasingly popular, particularly in colleges where young people had left their teenage years and were looking for a music that seemed genuine, avoiding the glossy production values of the teen records, and that had some sort of serious message. However, the raw sounds of roots folk singers were transformed into a smooth listening experience with groups such as The Kingston Trio ('Where Have All The Flowers Gone?', 1961) and Peter, Paul and Mary ('If I Had A Hammer', 1962; 'Puff The Magic Dragon', 1963).

Dancing the twist

MUSICAL EXAMPLE

NEIL SEDAKA, 'HAPPY BIRTHDAY SWEET SIXTEEN' (1961)

The original release of this classic pop song featured an orchestral accompaniment with soaring strings that occasionally played **pizzicato** motifs between phrases.

Pizzicato: Plucked.

G/D: When there are two chords separated by a right leaning slash in this way, the first letter represents the chord and the second the bass note – in this case, a G chord with a D in the bass.

Sequence: When music is repeated a number of times at a higher or lower pitch. In this case the rhythm changes slightly so I have used the term 'melodic sequence'.

Parallel 3rds: These make a sweet-sounding harmony and make the texture fuller. When using them, check that they fit with the harmony.

Semitone: The smallest step in pitch on a keyboard, for example from C to C♯.

Piano, bass and drums for a rhythm section lead into the opening nonsense vocals Tra-la-la-la-la la-la-la-la sung in harmonies for four bars then repeated.

The song itself uses a great many chords known technically as secondary dominants. These are where a chord is a V^7 chord in relation to the chord that follows, but not in the key of the piece. Thus A^7 is a secondary dominant for D minor when in the key of the song is C major. They are marked with an asterisk in the chord progression of the main verse set out below.

Sheet music:

G | G | B^7 | B^7* | Em | Em | G^7 | G^7* | C | C♯dim | **G/D** | E^7* | A^7 | A^7* | D^7 | D^7 ||

Recording:

D♭ | D♭ | F^7 | F^7* | B♭m | B♭m | D♭^{7} | D♭^{7}* | G♭ | Gdim | D♭/A♭ | B♭^{7}* | E♭^{7} | E♭^{7}* | A♭^{7} | A♭^{7} ||

Note: although G major is the key in the published sheet music, the recording is in D♭ major. Presumably this was to make it easier for amateurs to both sing (as it is a lower key) and play.

The tune descends using an outline of a melodic **sequence** (shown by the letters in the music below) for eight bars with harmonies in **parallel 3rds** underneath, then rises and falls for another eight, ending on chord V:

0:36 The 16 bars are then repeated, ending this time on chord I with the pizzicato violins making an appearance.

1:01 A middle section takes us through A minor and, after some emphatic stops, returns us to the main tune for a final verse of 16 bars.

1:52 The music then changes key, going up a **semitone** (on the recording going from D♭ major to D major – a commonly used key change at this time, giving the music a lift at the end. It became known as the truck driver's modulation as the result sounded like moving up a gear. However, in later years it was seen as trite because of over-use.

Thus the structure is as follows:

Bass lead in	Tra la intro	Tra la intro	Verse ending on V	Verse ending on I	Middle section	Verse ending on I	Verse ending on I	Tra la ending	Tra la ending	Fade out
3 beats	4 bars	4 bars	16 bars	16 bars	16 bars	16 bars	16 bars	4 bars	4 bars	4+ bars

⇑
key change

PRODUCED ROCK AND ROLL

The simple and direct aspects of country music can be traced in the appeal of rock and roll. As the first wave of rockabilly stars faded slightly, others continued to produce hits well into the 1960s, partly because they fitted in with the professionally produced standards of the decade. The Everly Brothers ('All I Have To Do Is Dream', 1957; 'Cathy's Clown', 1960) summed up this sweeter sound with their two-part close-harmony singing and strummed steel-strung guitars. Roy Orbison also falls into this category ('Only The Lonely', 1960; 'Oh, Pretty Woman', 1964).

MUSICAL EXAMPLE

ROY ORBISON, 'OH, PRETTY WOMAN' (1964)

Roy Orbison

The song begins with driving downbeats from the drums over which is layered a solo electric guitar playing a riff made from the V^7 chord of A major (E^7), which gradually builds up the intro. At first it is based on three beats in a bar but then settles to a firm four to provide a solid beat.

0:15 After this tense build-up the music resolves onto progressions of chords I to vi repeated under the vocal entry, then six beats of IV leading to another long section on V^7: four with vocals, then four of the guitar riff while Orbison snarls 'Mercy!'

0:41 Verse 2 follows with a tiger-like growl to round it off.

1:08 A less aggressive middle section now provides contrast, with the vocals in descending sequence over the chords:

Dm | G^7 | C | Am | Dm | G^7 | C | C :|| A^7 |

50s progression: Chords I I VI I IV I V:|| or I I VI I II I V:||

1:39 The music gets even mellower as a section based around a **50s progression** in A leads us back to

1:50 the opening guitar riff and

1:59 a repeat of verse 1 and

2:09 repeats of the V^7 harmony for no fewer than 25 bars, with the guitar riff over the words 'She's walkin' back to me', building up and up until a dead stop, with two quick chords on 'woman' to finish.

The song is remarkable on three counts:

1. The driving tension of the guitar riff

2. Orbison's unusual bar structure and **time signatures**

3. A narrative interest (although this was not new: see, for example, The Coasters, 'Smokey Joes Café', 1955).

Roy Orbison became famous for his laid-back style and sunglasses.

Time signature: Indication of the number of beats in a bar. For example, $\frac{3}{4}$ = 3 crotchet beats in a bar.

THE RISE OF THE PRODUCER

Performing artists that were signed to the big record labels had little or no control over what song they were given to sing or how the record was produced. This was left to the 'professionals'. One famous songwriting team rose above the level of simply writing music and handing it to an A&R person. Lyricist Jerry Leiber and composer Mike Stoller wrote a huge number of hits during the 1950s and 60s, including songs for Elvis Presley, The Drifters and The Coasters. They even formed their own record company. The young singer Phil Spector was more interested in producing than performing, and he served an apprenticeship with Leiber and Stoller in New York; when he set off on his own he became one of the most influential producers of the time.

Phil Spector in the studio

Phil Spector's technique was to put large numbers of musicians into a small space, flooding the sound they produced with artificial **reverberation** and echo and producing a mono backing track, over which he would layer his lead vocalists' recordings. The result was an impressive full tone that became known as 'the wall of sound'. He believed that it was the production not the singers that were the stars. However, many groups benefitted from his technique, including The Righteous Brothers ('You've Lost That Lovin' Feelin'', 1964), and Ike and Tina Turner ('River Deep – Mountain High', 1966). In the early years of the 1960s he specialised in girl groups, such as The Crystals ('Da-Doo-Ron-Ron', 'Then He Kissed Me', both 1963) and The Ronettes ('Baby, I Love You', 1963).

Reverberation (reverb): The effect of multiple echoes created in a large space by complex reflections, for example in a cathedral. Reverb can also be produced artificially by electrical signals applied to springs or metal sheets (plates) or by digital means.

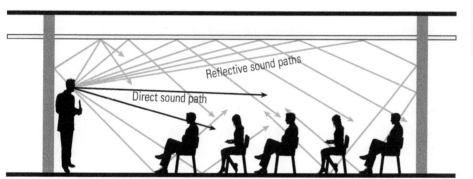

After sound has ended at the source, the sound wave will continue to reflect off of surfaces until the sound wave loses energy by absorption until it eventually dies out. This is called reverberation. Adapted from www.baswaphon.com

MUSICAL EXAMPLE

THE CRYSTALS, 'DA-DOO-RON-RON' (1963)

Harmonically simple – just three chords – this song still has enormous impact. This is partly due to Phil Spector's recording techniques. In his relatively small room in Gold Star Studios, Hollywood, he packed in several grand pianos and drum kits with bass players, strings and horns. Listen carefully to the backing track (www.youtube.com/watch?v=FsXkjmkm6EI) and you can hear powerful baritone sax parts doubling the bass and high triplet figures on the pianos. The whole instrumentation was put through an echo chamber where speakers played back the sound at one end of a room and microphones picked it up at the other. Spector would get his musicians to play it over and over until he achieved the sound in his head.

There is a four-bar intro establishing E♭ major and the fast triplet time signature.

0:06 Verse 1: eight bars of vocals, a simple three-note tune powerfully projected by the three girl singers over E♭ | A♭ | B♭ | E♭:|| The 'ron-rons' of the lyrics are set to a fast-moving **offbeat**.

0:19 Chorus (although the lyrics are different each time it returns I have named it as a chorus because of its memorable impact), eight bars, featuring the vocal entry on an accented second beat, and two-bar repeated phrases with snare fills between.

0:32 At the end of the chorus is a two-bar link with heavy snare triplet fills, and slack-tuned floor tom drums playing cross-rhythms:

0:35 Verse 2, chorus and two-bar link.

1:04 Sax solo for eight bars.

1:17 Verse 3, chorus and two-bar link.

1:46 **Coda** repeating the song title words, leading to a fade-out.

Offbeats: The second and fourth beats of a bar.

Coda: A section at the end of a song used to finish things off.

INSTRUMENTAL GROUPS

In the early 1960s there was a brief fashion for instrumental groups. In the USA The Ventures were on the way to becoming the best-selling instrumental group of all time. They used Fender guitars – the bright Stratocaster lead guitar, a warmer sounding Jazzmaster and a Precison Bass. In the UK Hank Marvin of The Shadows, originally The Drifters and Cliff Richard's backing group, owned the first Stratocaster in the country. The group had a number of hits at this time ('Apache', 1960; 'Wonderful Land', 1962; 'The Rise And Fall Of Flingel Bunt', 1964). Marvin's guitar techniques included a clear but reverberated sound, sometimes using tape echo and the use of the tremolo arm to produce vibrato; as a contrast he would also mute the vibrations with his palm to produce a more muffled and clicky tone.

MUSICAL INSTRUMENT

THE GUITAR

The guitar has six strings tuned to:

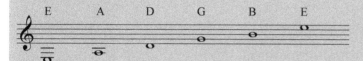

These are known as open strings. Additional notes are obtained by stopping the strings with fingers on the frets, thin strips of metal embedded in the fingerboard. All notes sound an octave lower than written. Sometimes guitars use a system called tab, which is a more graphic representation of the notes than traditional notation. For example:

The notes here are placed on the standard stave

The notes here are placed on six lines for the six strings with numbers to indicate on which frets to place the fingers.

Players use a number of ways to sound the strings: strumming, picking with fingertips, picking with a plectrum, hammer-ons and pull-offs. These last two involve the left hand (for a right-handed player) sounding the strings by fretting a note and respectively hammering down hard or plucking with another finger of the same hand. Pitch bends can be achieved by pulling strings across the fretboard or with a tremolo arm (misnamed as tremolo normally refers to a fluctuation in volume not pitch) attached to the bridge.

High chords that do not use open strings are achieved by pressing the first finger across the fretboard. These are called barré chords. For keys that require large numbers of barré chords (such as B♭ or E♭) players sometimes use a **capo**, especially when playing an acoustic guitar where the sonority of open strings may be required for finger-picking folk styles.

Capo: Short for *capo tasto*, this is a device that clamps across the fretboard of a guitar, raising the pitch.

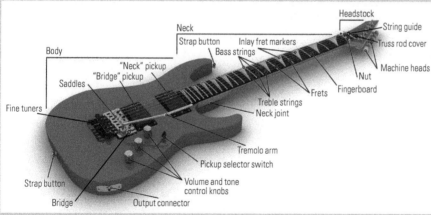

The parts of an electric guitar

Electric guitars use a variety of pickups. These are coils of fine wire round a magnet that pick up the vibrations of the metal strings and convert the disturbances of the magnetic field into electrical energy. The movement of a diaphragm in a microphone works in the same way. Most guitars have three pickups, in different positions under the strings, with the ability to be controlled individually, thus producing varying tones. Different gauges (weights) of strings are available, with rock players preferring light gauge (which are easier to bend) and jazz players heavy gauge (which give a richer sound).

Square wave: Electrical oscillation (fluctuation) that is characterised by being suddenly on, then held, then suddenly off. Used by synthesisers to produce a hollow-sounding tone.

Other instrumentals of the time included the Tornados' hit 'Telstar', named after a communications satellite, which featured a memorable tune played on a Clavioline, a precursor of the synthesiser popular with gigging musicians for its portability. It would attach to the underside of a piano keyboard providing the player with a choice of monophonic sounds for melodic lines. Its sound was characterised by a buzzing **square wave** with an insistent vibrato, and its volume was controlled by the player's right knee (see the excellent article at www.soundonsound.com/sos/mar07/articles/clavioline.htm).

BEAT MUSIC

By the time The Beatles released their first single 'Love Me Do' in October 1962, a bluesy beat number that reached number 17 in the UK charts, they were already very experienced performers. They had played night after night in the Cavern Club in Liverpool and toured to Hamburg. In Germany they had met a number of influential US rock and roll singers (including Little Richard) and been influenced by their techniques. The following year (1963) their second single 'Please, Please Me' reached number 1. The Beatles style typified the music coming out of Liverpool at the time, which became known as Merseybeat. Beat music was a fusion of styles – particularly rock and roll, R&B and soul – and it is even possible to trace a doo-wop influence, as many bands were fond of close harmonies. It was characterised by strong rhythms with unswung straight quavers, catchy tunes and a guitar-dominated line-up of lead, rhythm and bass plus drums. There had been a few home-grown acts in Britain from 1960 to 1962, particularly Elvis-influenced singers such as Tommy Steele, Billy Fury and Cliff Richard: rock and roll performers popular with teenagers. Now the new 1963 sounds of the Liverpool Cavern Club reached a wider audience, not just being played on **Radio Luxembourg** but even reaching the stage of Royal Variety Performance. Following the success of The Beatles, the UK charts were for the first time dominated by British bands – the table below shows some of the big hits of 1963.

Radio Luxembourg: A commercial radio station broadcasting to Britain from Europe to avoid the legal monopoly held at that time by the BBC. It is now known as RTL.

Released	Group	Song title
February	The Beatles	'Please, Please Me'
March	Gerry and the Pacemakers	'How Do You Do It?'
May	Gerry and the Pacemakers	'I Like It'
June	The Searchers	'Sweets For My Sweet'
August	Freddie and the Dreamers	'I'm Telling You Now'
August	The Hollies	'Stay'
November	The Dave Clarke Five	'Glad All Over'
December	The Swinging Blue Jeans	'The Hippy, Hippy Shake'

THE BEATLES, 'SHE LOVES YOU' (1963)

The song begins with an eight-bar intro based on repeated two-bar phrases of the title lyrics together with the famous unison 'Yeah, yeah, yeah's. The intro ends on an added sixth chord (G^6) in vocal harmony and a short guitar fill. McCartney's dotted-rhythm bass helps to add movement.

0:12 The melody of verse 1 begins with a rising two-bar scale adopting two-part harmony on its last note and continuing with a balancing two-bar phrase that is mostly in thirds. This four bars of music then repeats, leading to

0:24 the title lyrics for an eight-bar section with three strummed lead guitar chords dividing the 4+4. The structure of phrases for the verse is therefore 2+2+2+2+4+4 bars.

0:34 The verse is repeated to different lyrics, this time ending with The Beatles' trademark high 'Ooh's in thirds.

1:03 The two-bar material of the introduction returns but is now extended with three emphasised crotchets on 'love like that' over a minor chord IV (C minor), a chord often used by The Beatles to add colour.

1:16 Verse 3.

1:54 An extended coda, at first emphasising the 'love like that' crotchets, repeating the phrases and then coming to a halt with a turn on 'should' in thirds. It concludes with the 'Yeah, yeah, yeah's, repeated to end on another G^6 chord.

This song was a huge success for The Beatles and defined the Merseybeat sound. The unison 'Yeah, yeah, yeah's, the tasteful guitar licks and above all the character of the vocal harmonies helped make the song the band's best-selling single in the UK.

The Beatles produced hit after hit during the 1960s and spearheaded what became known as the 'British Invasion'. In 1964, despite initial reservations, they were persuaded by their manager, Brian Epstein, to cross the Atlantic to appear on the Ed Sullivan TV show. With a US number-one hit song ('I Want To Hold Your Hand') to help, their appearance was a sensation and they became household names overnight. They dominated the US charts from 1964 to 1966 (the group held 12 positions in the *Billboard* Hot 100 singles chart during one week in April 1964, including the top five positions – a feat that has not been matched by any other artist to date). Naturally, this encouraged a number of British artists to follow them to capitalise on their success. A selection of British bands to achieve number-one hits in the USA is given below:

Year	Artist	Single
1964	Manfred Mann	'Do Wah Diddy Diddy'
	The Animals	'House Of The Rising Sun'
1965	Freddie and the Dreamers	'I'm Telling You Now'
	Wayne Fontana and the Mindbenders	'Game Of Love'
	Herman's Hermits	'Mrs Brown, You've Got A Lovely Daughter'
	The Rolling Stones	'(I Can't Get No) Satisfaction'
1966	The Troggs	'Wild Thing'
	Donovan	'Sunshine Superman'

Two female vocalists to have particular success in the USA during this time should also be mentioned: Dusty Springfield ('I Only Want To Be With You', 1963) and Petula Clarke ('Downtown', 1964). The latter was also very popular in Europe.

For many years one of the few ways British teenagers could hear and see rock and roll performed was through imported US films at the cinema. Now the situation was reversed. The Beatles film *A Hard Day's Night* (1964) was met with much critical acclaim and was swiftly followed by *Help!* (1965), both films spawning music albums of 11 tracks. The films added to The Beatles' popularity in the USA as well as the UK and played a part in the British Invasion. We will examine the track 'Ticket To Ride' from *Help!* in more detail.

MUSICAL EXAMPLE

THE BEATLES, 'TICKET TO RIDE' (1965)

Paul McCartney said the title of the song referred to a train ticket to Ryde on the Isle of Wight. The song begins with a 12-string Rickenbacker guitar playing a riff that could be interpreted as the motion of a train as it crosses over the tracks.

When Ringo introduces the drumbeat in the third bar it is anything but an orthodox rhythm. It has a tambourine off-beat and partly doubles the 12-string guitar riff, with an emphasis halfway through the third beat, making the sound even more like train tracks.

Double tracking: Where a sound is recorded on one track and then recorded a second time on another. Usually applied to vocals to strengthen their sound in a mix. It was difficult for the artists as they had to sing the music exactly the same both times, but in the late 1960s the process was automated electronically (known as ADT: automatic double tracking, or artificial double tracking).

0:07 The melody line of John Lennon's **double-tracked** vocals rises and falls as we travel, with the highest note being a blues 7th (G♯). The verse is made from regular phrases: four bars, four bars, then four times two bars that bring out the song title.

0:38 Verse 2 repeats verse 1 with different lyrics.

1:09 A middle section follows with two times four bars, plus an extension bar of guitar lead, delaying the return of the verse and increasing its effectiveness.

1:26 The third verse then repeats the music and lyrics of verse 2.

1:58 The middle section then returns, complete with its extension bar.

2:15 The third verse then repeats the music and lyrics of verse 2.

2:47 There then follows an extended coda fade-out to the words 'My baby don't care', with percussion and 12-string guitar providing a double-tempo feel, almost as if the train is shooting off into the distance.

'Ticket To Ride' therefore uses a standard AABA structure with some important differences:

1. The B section is extended by one bar from eight to nine bars.
2. After the music has completed its first complete structure it returns straight away to the B section rather than the A.
3. There is an extended coda to finish off the song.

While The Beatles were influenced by rockabilly and groups such as Buddy Holly and The Crickets, others such as The Zombies, The Kinks and The Rolling Stones used blues and R&B as their main inspiration. The Zombies' first hit 'She's Not There' fared better in the USA than the UK, reaching number 2 in the *Billboard* charts.

MUSICAL EXAMPLE

THE ZOMBIES, 'SHE'S NOT THERE' (1964)

Tierce de Picardie: A effect in harmony when music is in a minor key and the last chord is suddenly major.

Distortion: An effect used to add warmth and thickness to a sound. Nowadays it is produced electronically, but in the 1950s and 60s musicians used to physically damage their amplifiers, or send such a high signal into them that the electronic circuitry would overload, producing a garbled sound. Engineers produced gadgets called fuzz-boxes to do the same job. Dave Davies' guitar solo in 'You Really Got Me' was distorted because of cuts made to his speaker cone.

This song seems to be in a minor key. Technically it moves between two modes: the Dorian and the Aeolian. Modes are 'scales' that can be played using just the white notes of the keyboard, and are traceable back to before medieval times. The music staves below show the notes of the Aeolian mode, and the Dorian mode transposed to start on the song's key note of A, together with the original D-starting Dorian mode. The electric keyboard (Hohner Pianet played by Rod Argent) moves freely between the two modes, creating a moody jazz sound.

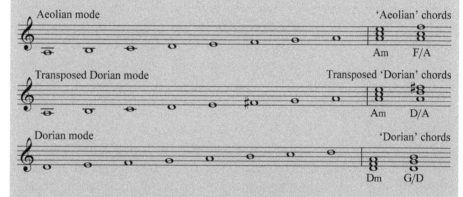

The song begins with a smooth melodic bass with drums, playing a Latin-derived rhythm of

This economical but effective pattern continues right through to the chorus. At the end of the verse a G# is introduced (0:33), producing a chord V which makes us think for the first time of A minor, but the chorus continues the modal harmony. Furthermore, on the last chord of the chorus (0:46) the A minor key chord is changed to A major. This is called a *tierce de Picardie*, an effect more common in classical music.

The Kinks were a band from North London and were formed by two brothers, Ray and Dave Davies, in 1964. Their early singles were influenced by R&B and featured the use of parallel-finger sliding barré chords: 'You Really Got Me' (August 1964) used adjacent chords of F and G in the pattern FGGFG, and 'All Day And All Of The Night' (October 1964) used FG GF FB♭B♭B♭G. The heavy sound they produced, together with Dave's bluesy **distorted** guitar solos, set the scene for many heavy metal bands to come. Their later output showcased the songwriting talents of Ray, for example the wistful 'Waterloo Sunset' (1967).

The Kinks

Black-influenced music: Other bands that adopted The Rolling Stones' black-influenced approach include The Animals ('House Of The Rising Sun', 1964) and The Yardbirds ('For Your Love', 1965 – although this was a more pop-style track, which forced their lead guitarist Eric Clapton to leave them and join John Mayall and the Bluesbreakers, a more R&B-based band).

The Rolling Stones, another London band, were also **influenced by black US music**, particularly the Delta and Chicago blues styles, even using harmonica and slide guitar. They cultivated a contrasting image to The Beatles, more rebellious with longer hair, and would undo their ties from time to time if they had to wear suits. They were the bad boys of the neighbourhood. The lead singer, Mick Jagger, had a powerful visual presence, and the band used this to project their rhythmic rock style. The band's early singles were all cover versions, particularly of blues singers such as Muddy Waters and Bo Diddley. It is a useful exercise to compare their version of 'Not Fade Away' with Buddy Holly's original. They were friends with The Beatles, although several years younger, and even recorded a song written by Lennon and McCartney ('I Wanna Be Your Man', 1963).

MUSICAL EXAMPLE

THE ROLLING STONES, 'I CAN'T GET NO (SATISFACTION)' (1965)

The Rolling Stones

The song features a strong two-bar lead guitar riff, used in the introduction and chorus sections, that rises from the fifth note of the scale up to the flattened blues seventh.

0:14 Mick Jagger's sultry vocals enter in a low register over a verse that alternates between chords of E and A at first, but then introduces a B⁷ as he repeats the words 'and I try', joined by the rest of the band. This leads to

0:34 a chorus where the high E E G♯ E setting of 'I can't get no' repeats for emphasis and the guitar riff is re-introduced. The high E is used to declame the next set of lyrics for ten bars, and the chorus lyrics are repeated, leading to

1:02 solo drums for two bars that pound out the four-in-a-bar heavy beats.

1:05 Vocals return with 'Hey, hey, hey, what'd I say?'

1:14 Verse 2, followed by a repeat of the chorus.

2:13 Verse 3 and a repeat of the chorus.

3:14 A coda section repeating the title lyrics and leading to a fade-out.

The song is very effective because of its driving beat, the famous guitar riff that combined with the repeated chord I to chord IV harmonies, and Jagger's delivery of the lyrics, which were controversial enough in their day to delay a UK release.

DEVELOPMENTS IN THE USA

Corporate music in the USA had had something of a culture shock when The Beatles, and the bands that crossed the Atlantic in their wake, met with so much success. There were many US imitators keen to cash in on the craze, including bands such as The Monkees (a band that was put together for a TV show), who were seen as the industry's answer to The Beatles – four loveable lads who went down well with the mums and dads.

Across college campuses in the USA and throughout arty urban areas such as Greenwich Village in New York, music fans had not forgotten their grass roots. The folk-music scene was thriving, influenced by acoustic performers such as Woodie Guthrie and Pete Seeger.

In the early 1960s Bob Dylan arrived in Greenwich Village from his native Minnesota. He was more well known as a songwriter and poet than a performer, although he quickly gained a reputation as a powerful communicator. He had a number of the songs from his albums covered to great success by other artists (such as 'Blowin' In The Wind', covered by Peter, Paul and Mary in 1963: the band shared the same manager as Dylan). In January 1965 The Byrds had a huge hit with his 'Mr Tambourine Man' and started off the whole folk-rock genre. Using electric guitars and close-harmony singing, they turned Dylan's folk song into a rock number. In 1965 they gave folk singer Pete Seeger's composition 'Turn, Turn, Turn' a similar treatment.

In July 1965, Dylan appeared in the Newport Folk Festival wielding an electric guitar, which outraged many of the traditionalist folk fans. Gradually Dylan produced more and more numbers with electric instruments, and his singles crossed over to the pop charts. 'Like A Rolling Stone' was released in July of 1965, just after Dylan had returned from a successful but gruelling tour of the UK.

MUSICAL EXAMPLE

BOB DYLAN, 'LIKE A ROLLING STONE' (1965)

This song's lyrics don't deal with the usual theme of teenage love, but are much more desolate, describing a young woman who is alone and down on her luck, fallen from a rich girl's position of privilege to that of a scrounger. The song is remarkable for its length – over six minutes – creating initial difficulties with its release.

The music is indeed electric, with electric bass and rhythm guitar and a Hammond organ, the latter playing memorable lead fills during the chorus. There is a full drum set and tambourine, and Dylan retains his trademark harmonica (although reduced to only a few interjections at the end of the choruses) with his forceful vocal tone enunciating lyrics following the natural rhythms of the poetry. The instrumentation is fuller than Dylan usually used, but the sense of formal control is eased by the overall sound of several musicians jamming along.

0:11 The verse begins with Dylan's vocals chanting out a repeated C key note, with the question 'didn't you?' rising higher in pitch at the end of the phrase. During this the guitar plays a simple rising scale based on the harmonies and lifting the mood.

0:20 The same happens again for the next line of verse.

0:30 The verse then moves to a section of F and G harmonies with shorter phrases in the lyrics followed by four bars with the guitar playing a descending scale ready for four bars that end with an emphasised chord V (G), to act as a build-up for:

1:00 the eight-bar chorus 'How does it feel?', which is powerfully climactic, Dylan frequently coming in ahead of the beat in eager anticipation.

1:20 There then follows a short instrumental interlude featuring organ and harmonica before the second verse.

The structure is a simple verse/chorus form, with four verses altogether, the last chorus extended to ten bars by repeating the last phrase with the instrumental interlude being used as a fade-out.

The song had a strong influence on many artists, including The Beatles and Bruce Springstein.

R&B STUDIOS: MOTOWN AND STAX

Solo artists such as soul singer Ray Charles and pop ballad crooner Nat King Cole were producing major hits in the early 1960s. US R&B changed as the decade progressed, adopting the high production and presentation standards of the mainstream. Two studios met with particular success: Motown in Detroit and Stax in Memphis.

The Motown label was created by Berry Gordy in 1960 (his second label – the first was Tamla, founded in 1959) and employed exclusively black musicians, artists and producers in its Detroit studios (although some backing tracks were imported from California, where white musicians were employed). Gordy knew there was serious money to be made if he could produce black music that could cross over from the R&B charts to the pop charts. He employed a house band nicknamed the Funk Brothers on almost all the label's records from 1959 to 1972, which was made up of a variety of expert session musicians. Artists were groomed to be inoffensive. Girl groups would appear on TV in evening gowns and the men all wore suits, singing lyrics strictly controlled to avoid suggestive language.

Music production values were high, and as well as the Funk Brothers backing group strings and brass were frequently employed. Violins played high, sustained harmony lines and brass provided punchy rhythms. However, this type of music can be categorised as soul, which emphasises the voice above instrumental techniques, so there were few sections of instrumental virtuosity.

bpm: Beats per minute. For example, 120 bpm = two beats per second.

Downbeats: The first and third beats of a bar.

Motown songs did not often use the blues idiom. More typically they would adopt the AABA of mainstream jazz and Tin Pan Alley styles. Their tempi were usually set at 120 **bpm** or above, and studio engineers would mix for the transistor radio in mind, emphasising upper frequencies with tambourines and high hats in the forefront. Bass lines would be rhythmically inventive and drums would stress the **downbeats** with extra percussion added, often a tambourine.

The studio's first major hit was by The Miracles ('Shop Around', 1960) with their lead vocalist Smokey Robinson. Below is a list of some of hits to come out of the studio during the first half of the decade.

Released	Group	Song title
1960	The Miracles	'Shop Around'
1961	The Marvelettes	'Please Mr Postman'
1964	The Supremes	'Where Did Our Love Go?'
1964	The Supremes	'Baby Love'
1964	Martha and the Vandellas	'Dancing In The Street'
1964	Marvin Gaye	'How Sweet It Is'
1964	Mary Wells	'My Guy'
1964	The Temptations	'My Girl'
1965	The Supremes	'Stop! In The Name Of Love'
1965	The Miracles	'The Tracks Of My Tears'

MUSICAL INSTRUMENT
THE HAMMOND ORGAN

- 88 8800 00: 'Green Onions'
- 88 0808 000: 'Whiter Shade Of Pale'
- 00 5644 320 : small church organ
- 32 7645 222: cathedral organ

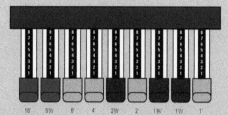

Drawbars

This electronic organ had been around since the 1930s, but it came into its own during the 1950s and 60s. It started life as a church organ but, partly because of the innovative way it produced its sound, found its way into other fields of music. The B3 model was used first as a jazz instrument, with players such as Jimmy Smith creating exciting instrumental blues and **bebop** albums, then it moved into pop music. Booker T and the MGs had a memorable hit with 'Green Onions' (1962), which featured an organ playing lead for a simple 12-bar blues, and the instrument was used by the band Procul Harum to play a famous Bach-like lead verse for their 1967 hit 'A Whiter Shade Of Pale'. It was also a favourite instrument for the US west-coast surf style and the heavy rock bands of the 1970s.

It employs a series of drawbars mounted across the top of the console, coloured black, brown and white. The white ones are tuned to the notes you would expect but in different octaves, so if you played C, a C note would be produced, its octave and volume level depending on which of the black drawbars was extended and how far it was pulled out. The other drawbars were tuned to other notes of the harmonic series (see p. 58) and were used to colour the sound, so that if large numbers of these were extended the tone would become more nasal.

Popular settings, where 8 is fully out, include:

- 88 8000 008: gospel sound
- 88 5324 588: blues sound

This way of producing new sounds by adding the sine waves of various pitches is known technically as additive synthesis. The organ also included 'harmonic percussion', which was the facility of providing an emphasised envelope (see p. 58) to a note so that it decayed quickly. This allowed players to emulate a the sound of instruments that have a quick decay at the start of their notes, such as piano or guitar. Unlike these acoustic instruments, however, the effect would only be repeated when all the notes of a chord, or set of legato notes had been released, allowing in the hands of expert players some very expressive effects.

The instrument featured two manuals (keyboards) plus two octaves of notes played by foot pedals. The normal way of playing would be to set the sound of the top manual and use it with the right hand as the lead part, while setting the sound quieter for the left hand to use as an accompaniment on the lower manual. Expression could also be achieved with a right-foot 'swell' control (the left foot being occupied with the bass pedals).

Although the organ had a built-in amplifier and speaker, the sound was often sent through a Leslie cabinet. This was an external amplifier and speaker which contained a rotating horn, with the player having the choice a fast (tremolo) or slow (chorale). This projected the sound out using the physics of the **Doppler effect** to create a characteristic slight shift in pitch.

Bebop: A small-group jazz style in quick tempo, with improvisations based on the harmonic structure of a standard song but employing a more chromatic language with unusual phrasing.

Doppler effect: A phenomenon where the sound waves of a moving object arrive more quickly as their source approaches a listener than when it is moving away, which changes the pitch the listener hears: for example, the changing pitch of a siren as a fire engine drives past.

MUSICAL EXAMPLE

THE SUPREMES, 'BABY LOVE' (1964)

The Supremes were made up of three girl singers: Diana Ross, the lead, with Florence Ballard and Mary Wilson providing backing and ad-lib vocals. The song was written and produced by Motown's own team, comprising the brothers Brian and Edward Holland plus Lamont Dozier (known as Holland-Dozier-Holland or H-D-H). The house band The Funk Brothers provided the backing, but often would not appear with the girls on TV – mostly performances were lip-synched (in other words, the singers would mime to a playback of the recording).

The song begins with a short intro which sets the shuffle rhythm and leads into Diana Ross singing a four-note 'Ooh' as a vocal break.

0:08   The first verse begins with the words of the song title and continues with a strong four-in-a-bar beat, a descending dotted rhythm bass line and high piano chords.

0:17   There follow three insistent two-bar phrases listing the poor ways the singers are treated by their lover, finishing with an emphatic crotchet statement for 'to make you stay away so long'.

0:30   The music then repeats for a second verse, with the backing singers providing comment: 'Don't throw our love away!'

0:51   There begins what seems to be third verse, but after a four bars it is taken over by an instrumental break featuring a sax solo leading to

1:12   another verse of 12 bars, leading to

1:34   two bars of instrumental serving as a modulation or transition (music that changes key) from C to D♭ – up a semitone.

The new key is established and then two more verses with a fuller accompaniment including the lead sax lead to a fade-out to finish the song.

The music is therefore in simple verse form, helping the catchy tune become embedded in the listener's consciousness.

Diana Ross and the Supremes

Diana Ross and The Supremes and many other bands continued the success of the Motown label through the rest of the 1960s and into the next decade. The most popular track the studio produced and to some its most impressive was Marvin Gaye's 'I Heard It Through The Grapevine', released in 1966.

Another record label that managed to produce a number of R&B songs to chart in the pop charts was Stax records of Memphis, which formed a partnership with Atlantic Records in 1961. Southern soul is typified by music that was often slightly more laid back, with slower tempi and less glossy production. The music was less close-miked than Motown, with more distance placed between the musicians and the listener. Stax's biggest star was the soul singer Otis Redding ('Sittin' On The Dock Of The Bay', 1968), who with the backing band of Booker T and the MGs produced a more heartfelt sound than the smooth sounds coming out of Detroit.

Listeners in the UK designated Tamla-Motown and southern soul as 'hip', but sometimes were surprised by the slightly staged performances when they saw the performers on the TV. The second half of the decade was to bring even more surprises.

CHAPTER 3

The 1960s (part 2)

BACKGROUND

A mixture of optimism and cynicism characterised the attitudes of young people as the 1960s progressed. The cynicism concerned disillusionment with the institutions of the state and some of the commonly held values of society. Some sought utopian escapes, imaginary lands full of beautiful people, a nirvana where they would be untouched by the stress and strain of daily life. Taking drugs, moving away from home to life in communes and listening to spacey music were all ways of coping. The hit song 'San Francisco (Be Sure To Wear Some Flowers In Your Hair)' (1967) by Scott McKenzie encouraged young people from the West Coast of the USA to attend the Monterey Pop Festival, which in turn led to the so-called Summer of Love, where they would find a new freedom and fresh experiences.

Optimism showed itself through a consumerist approach to life. London was fast becoming the fashion capital of the world, temporarily taking over from Paris. Fashion designers such as Mary Quant, models such as Twiggy and areas of London such as Carnaby Street contributed to the concept of 'swinging London'. The Kinks' hit single 'Dedicated Follower Of Fashion' (1966) summed it all up, making fun of the excesses of the time.

A series of youth styles developed from the mods and rockers of the UK and the working-class skinheads that came later, to the hippies of San Francisco. Members of the British mod movement would wear smart suits and parkas when riding on their Vespa motor scooters, laden with extra wing mirrors. Their favourite music was soul, Jamaican ska and British beat, with bands like The Who acting as their heroes.

London fashion in the 1960s

THE WHO

The Who appeared on a regular basis at the London club 'The Scene' in Soho and at the Marquee Club, whose tiny stage played host to almost every major rock band of the time. They toured the UK and the USA with a stage act that was both lively and destructive, smashing up their instruments at the end of a set. Their membership comprised Roger

A 1960s mod

Daltrey (lead vocals), Pete Townshend (guitar, piano and backing vocals – who wrote most of their material), John Entwistle (bass and backing vocals) and Keith Moon (drums). The band's recordings were frequently played on the pirate station Radio Caroline, including 'My Generation', a song which represented a feeling of youthful rebellion.

MUSICAL EXAMPLE

THE WHO, 'MY GENERATION' (1965)

The Who

The shape of the first vocal line is common in African-American styles and known as a 'shout and fall', or 'tumble refrain'.

The music is in an aggressive, up-tempo blues beat style with modal melody lines. These use the minor pentatonic (five-note) scale, which when set against the G major harmonies create the blues idiom:

Minor pentatonic on G

The song begins with a four-bar intro establishing the key of G with the flattened 7th in the bass, emphasising the modal blues; the intro ends with a lead-in triplet drum fill.

The vocals enter with a powerful high note that works its way down to a flat 3rd, followed immediately by the other group members singing the song title in 3rds. This call-and-response continues through the verse.

The second phrase is set lower as a contrast:

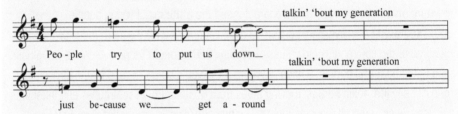

The two phrases then repeat with the new lyrics.

The lyrics for the verse are:

> People try to put us d-down (Talkin' 'bout my generation)
> Just because we g-g-get around (Talkin' 'bout my generation)
> Things they do look awful c-c-cold (Talkin' 'bout my generation)
> I hope I die before I get old (Talkin' 'bout my generation)
> My generation, My generation Baby.

0:29 Verse 2. This begins with the vocals set low and the controversial lyrics 'Why don't you all fff… fade away'.

Feedback: an effect common with inexperienced users of microphones, but guitar pickups can also produce the same result. It occurs when the speaker that the amplified sound comes from is placed too close to the pickup where the sound is captured, resulting in a sonic loop back round the system, creating strange howling noises. In this case the normally unwanted effect is being used deliberately for creative purposes.

0:54 The music continues with four lots of four-bar stop-time solos for the bass guitar (very unusual for the time), and a four-bar guitar solo to finish this instrumental section.

1:18 Now the music moves up a tone to the key of A (a 'truck driver's modulation' – see p. 21) and repeats the music with the lyrics for verse 2. After a four-bar instrumental extension it moves up again (1:42), this time to B♭, with four more bars of instrumental leading to:

1:47 a repeat of the opening verse.

2:16 The music moves up again, this time to C, and there begins a rather chaotic extended coda with triplet snare drums and electrical **feedback** from the guitar.

THE WEST-COAST SCENE

While much of the music business in the USA was centred in the east of the country, together with the northern industrial cities, there was a good deal of activity in California. In the early 1960s there was a style of music based on life on the beach, known as surf music. It included instrumental styles with heavily reverbed lead guitars or solo saxophones, and vocal groups such as The Beach Boys. When The Beatles were taking the country by storm in 1964, The Beach Boys had a number 1 hit with 'I Get Around'. By 1966 the group had had a series of hits and had toured extensively without Brian Wilson, the member of the band who wrote their music, who in December 1964 made the decision to stay at home so he would have more time to work on new songs. This was partly because of a desire to produce even better music fuelled by a friendly rivalry with The Beatles. He would create the backing tracks and then take them to the studio for the rest of the band to **overdub** the vocals. The studio-based approach was increasingly necessary as the group's music became ever more complicated.

Sixties surf culture

Overdub: Record music on a new track while listening to the music on other tracks. Frequent overdubbing is known as layering.

One of the most successful instrumental singles in the surf rock style was 'Wipeout' by The Surfaris (1963), which features driving semiquavers on the drum kit's tom toms. The term 'wipeout' referred to falling off a surfboard.

The Beach Boys' trade mark was close-harmony singing, influenced as much by doo-wop as by barber-shop styles, which when they combined it with rock and roll created an appealing sound. When The Beach Boys produced their album *Pet Sounds*, they broke new ground in pop music composition. The album featured a huge array of instruments and an inventive use of vocal textures.

Pet Sounds instrumentation

Guitars, both string bass and electric bass guitars, harpsichords, timpani, clarinets, glockenspiels, vibraphones, violins, violas, cellos, bongos, empty Coke bottles, ukuleles, flutes, French horns, cor anglais, tenor saxophones, baritone saxophones, bass clarinets, trumpets, accordions, organs, harmonicas, an electro-theremin and a piano.

Pet Sounds vocal textures

- Falsetto (very high male voice utilising a range above the normal mode, which produces a clear, flute-like sound used, for example, by Swiss yodellers)
- Homophonic (all parts using the same rhythm, creating block chords)
- Polyphonic (weaving independent parts)
- Antiphonal (answer phrases as in call-and-response)
- Lead vocal (the principal vocal)
- Backing vocal (accompanying vocal harmonies)
- Ostinato (a repeated pattern)
- A cappella (vocals with no instrumental accompaniment).

The Beach Boys

THE BEACH BOYS, 'GOOD VIBRATIONS' (1966)

Tenor range: One of the four main vocal ranges (soprano, alto, tenor and bass), and applying to a high male voice.

Baritone: Male vocal range lying between tenor and bass.

Electro-theremin: Sometimes described as the Tannerin, this is based on the early electronic instrument the theremin. The latter is played without physical contact, the instrument sensing the position of the player's hand between two antennae and producing ghostly sounds. The instrument was difficult to control and so the electro-theremin was introduced with a slider to control the pitch. The theremin was used famously in the soundtrack to Alfred Hitchcock's 1945 film *Spellbound*, music by Miklós Rózsa.

Triads: Three-note chords.

Chromatic: Using notes not in the key of the music, such as D♯ in G major. Music that stays in one key and doesn't use chromaticism is called diatonic. For examples of a more chromatic musical language than that used by The Beach Boys, see the analysis of 'Strawberry Fields Forever' on p. 43.

This single was written at the same time as the *Pet Sounds* album was being recorded, but released five months later. It features a number of interesting vocal textures, and an unusual construction, partly due to the fact that the last three sections were recorded separately and spliced together later.

The opening eight bars flow freely with reverberant vocals, repeated light organ chords and a bass guitar playing inventive patterns set high in the **tenor range**. Percussion comes in at bar 9 but not with a regular beat, all suiting the lyrics of sunlight and light breeze.

0:25 After 16 bars the chorus sets off with a stronger four-in-a-bar feel, and a **baritone** voice accompanied with triplets from keyboards, backing vocals and the strange-sounding **electro-theremin**. This instrument is clearly meant to represent the 'good vibrations' of the title, although the singer is getting them from the girl he is admiring.

0:38 The music moves up a tone for two bars from G♭ to A♭, the song's home key being E♭ minor.

0:45 The music moves up again, this time to B♭, which acts as chord V to E♭ minor, enabling a return to

0:51 verse 2, which repeats the music of verse 1 to new lyrics.

1:42 At the end of this verse there is an extended section of 20 bars, based on chord V (B♭), bars 13–16 of which are in E♭. This is the first of the spliced sections and adds an upright piano (with drawing pins pushed into the hammers for a more metallic sound), a jew's harp (a twangy spring in a frame held against the teeth that resonates according to the shape of the mouth), a bass harmonica and sleigh bells along with the voices, bass, tambourine and organ.

2:14 Then a completely new feel is introduced. The rhythm drops out and a church-like sustained organ sound holds chords of F, Gm and C.

2:57 Gradually the beat picks up as the kick drum enters with regular crotchets and then a high Cm⁷ vocal chord interrupts.

There follows repeats of the chorus material in various keys: B♭, A♭, G♭ going downwards, then back up again leading to:

3:14 a section of vocal counterpoint in contrary motion (one part goes up while another goes down), starting on a high falsetto rising scale with the voices coming in one after another.

3:26 The song then quickly fades out with the 'vibrations' ringing in our ears.

Despite the song's complexity, the harmonies are relatively straightforward. That is to say, the chords are all basic **triads**, with no strange added notes or **chromatic** movement. Nevertheless, the music is highly original with contrasting textures, changes in movement, ingenious instrumentation and an unusual structure.

There were several other US groups that specialised in sophisticated vocal arrangements. Another West Coast band, The Mamas and the Papas, had hits with 'California Dreamin'' (1965) and 'Monday, Monday' (1966), and The Four Seasons had 11 top-ten hits between 1962 and 1966 (such as 'Big Girls Don't Cry', 1962, and 'Rag Doll', 1964) led by the powerful falsetto voice of Frankie Valli. Equally famous for their smooth close-harmony singing was the folk-rock duo Simon and Garfunkel. Their first major hit was 'The Sound of Silence' (1964), which was featured in the comedy-drama film *The Graduate* (1967). Their album *Bookends* was number 1 on both sides of the Atlantic in 1968.

The Four Seasons had a hit musical play written about them called *Jersey Boys*. After its Broadway run it premiered in London's West End in 2008.

PSYCHEDELIC ROCK

Ever since the late 1950s there had gradually been in the clubs, shops and reading material in London and San Francisco a culture of experimentation with drugs. Writers such as Aldous Huxley (his book *The Doors of Perception*, 1954, details the effects of mescaline) and Timothy Leary (a former Harvard psychology lecturer who wrote encouragingly about the drug LSD) were interested in new ways people could experience the world. The Beatles were trying out LSD during their middle period. Their first album to reflect this was *Revolver* (1966), in particular tracks such as 'Tomorrow Never Knows'. This set lyrics such as 'Turn off your mind, relax and float down stream' – an almost exact quotation from Leary's writings. It also featured a tambura, an Indian long-necked stringed instrument designed to produce a rich, open-string drone, contributing to the dreamy sound and forcing static harmonies.

Music was composed under the influence of hallucinatory drugs or was written specifically to recreate the drug's experience, and the culture that surrounded this became known as 'psychedelia'. Similarly influenced psychedelic albums by The Beatles were *Sgt Pepper's Lonely Hearts Club Band* (1967), and *Magical Mystery Tour* (1968). The double-sided single 'Strawberry Fields Forever'/'Penny Lane' (1967) also falls into this category.

An example of a psychedelic album cover: King Crimson

Psychedelic Rock as a subgenre has a number of characteristics:

- Preference for album tracks so that music is not restrained by the short length of a single
- Use of exotic instruments, particularly from the Far East
- Increased use of keyboards in the studio, especially early synthesisers
- Use of more serious lyrics, often with surreal leanings
- A fondness for concept albums, where the tracks are linked in narrative form or at least based around a common theme
- Highly decorated album sleeves

■ Experimental recording studio techniques such as:

Technique	Description	
Heavy, spacy reverb and echo	Created by plate and spring reverbs, and the use of echo-chambers. It was the large amounts used by psychedelic rock musicians that was a feature of the style.	
ADT (automatic double tracking)	A tiny delay applied to a recording of a voice which, when combined with the original, makes it sound like two singers.	
Flanging	Whooshing sounds created by mixing two sounds together with one delayed by a gradually changing amount.	
Phasing	Sweeping effect created by mixing two sounds together with one treated by altering its waveform, creating interference between them.	
Overdrive, distortion and fuzz	Where the amplification system can't cope with the high levels of signal and so a woolly, indistinct or 'dirty' sound is produced.	
Tape manipulation techniques	Vari-speed recording	Recording at one speed and playing back at another changes the tone of the sound.
	Backwards playback	Playing back a section of tape the wrong way produces very unusual sounds: for example, a cymbal hit becomes a crescendo up to a sudden stop.
	Splicing	Sections of audio tape cut up with a razor blade and then stuck (spliced) together in a different order using special adhesive tape.
	Delay loops	Loops of tape producing various echo effects.
Panning effects	Sound moving between speakers; often tracks are **dual mono** rather than true stereo.	

Dual mono: Whereas stereo sound gives a sense of depth to audio by creating a two-dimensional field in the same way the human ear does, dual mono is simply different music in each of the two 'stereo' speakers.

WORKING IN THE STUDIO

As the decade progressed there was a general trend towards sophisticated album-based music, with advances in studio techniques, the technology of instruments and amplifiers and the skills of the performers involved. By 1966 The Beatles had abandoned touring and spent their time writing and recording in the studio. This enabled them to compose music that was highly original, freeing them from the limitations of performing live. George Martin, their producer, could read and write music notation and therefore was able to translate The Beatles' ideas concerning instrumentation into reality, hiring in strings and wind when required. (McCartney's 'Yesterday' from 1965 was the first Beatles track to use a 'classical' string quartet.) He was also able to work closely with EMI's engineers to harness new recording techniques to cope with Lennon and McCartney's fertile imaginations.

THE BEATLES, 'STRAWBERRY FIELDS FOREVER' (1967)

When John Lennon was a boy he lived near to a Salvation Army home for children and would often climb into its garden to play. It was named Strawberry Field.

The Beatles

A mellotron

John Lennon disliked the traditional double-tracking method whereby he would have to perform an identical version of his vocals for recording on another track. Double-tracking a vocal would make it much stronger in a mix and enable it to compete with heavy accompaniment.

Tag: A tag is where a musical phrase is repeated for the purposes of producing an emphasised ending.

The music begins with a short introduction composed by Paul McCartney, for what is essentially John Lennon's song. It is played on the unusual sounding Mellotron, a keyboard instrument that uses tape recordings of real instruments – in this case flutes.

One particular musical feature of the song is downward movement, perhaps representing the 'Let me take you down' lyrics. Lennon is seeking company for his dreamy 'trip' down memory lane. The lower part of the Mellotron introduction descends in step, the first three notes chromatically, the second three diatonically, totalling a perfect 5th.

0:10 The vocals enter, and at the end of the first line of lyrics there is a downward sliding feeling when the harmony changes to the chromatic chord of V minor, and another downward emphasis on 'fields' with a melodic falling 5th.

The lyrics are conversational rather than poetic, leading to some irregular phrase lengths and necessitating some time signature changes, 'Strawberry Fields forever' being delivered in $\frac{3}{4}$ time.

0:33 Verse 1 ('Living is easy with eyes closed'), using the Mellotron introduction as accompaniment.

0:54 Returning to the opening 'chorus', the instrumentation is enhanced by overdubbed semiquaver tom toms, cellos and brass. The word 'going' marks the point where two different recordings were spliced together. The pitch of the first half was moved up from A and the second down from C. George Martin managed to avoid a change in tempo in the finished version as the second half was originally performed faster, so the slower tape speed required for the key change worked out. (Nowadays this would be simple with digital technology.)

1:18 Linked to verse 2 by George Harrison playing the swarmandal (an Indian table harp, similar to a zither), the music moves steadily forwards with trumpets accompanying Lennon's double-tracked vocals (using the newly invented ADT processing). The tape of Ringo's percussion music is played backwards, making the high hats' crotchets sound 'scooping'.

1:41 The opening chorus then returns with an even fuller accompaniment, trumpets playing short repeated semiquaver interjections.

2:05 Verse 3 sees a dropping-out of some band instruments and more emphasis on the orchestral ones, cellos playing heavy crotchet triplets.

2:27 The next chorus using harmony vocals and leads to a coda.

2:47 The coda begins with a triple-time **tag** of the song title and leads to the electric lead guitar emphasising the flattened 7th, by moving a whole tone down from the key note (again a downward movement), and the music fades away with distant swarmandal notes and train-like semiquavers on the snare drum.

'Strawberry Fields Forever' was intended to be included on the album *Sgt Pepper's Lonely Hearts Club Band*, which was recorded immediately afterwards. This album continued the experimental recording techniques pioneered in *Revolver* and was also noted for its colourful record sleeve, which included the full text of the lyrics together with pictures of The Beatles dressed as members of the imaginary brass band. They were surrounded by images of famous people, including Karlheinz Stockhausen – a progressive, 'avant-garde' electronic composer whose compositions Paul McCartney had heard in London.

Techniques inspired by another avant-garde composer, Krzysztof Penderecki, were used on the track 'A Day In The Life'. John Lennon's four verses for this song required a contrasting middle section which was supplied by Paul ('Woke up, fell out of bed…') and at the end of John's third verse Paul also added the deliberately drug-related lyric 'I'd love to turn you on'. George Martin then acted on the composers' ideas and used the lyric and its undulating B/C quavers to morph into a huge orchestra crescendo, where the players made up their notes between supplied guides – in this case they would slide between given notes on their scores (a procedure known as aleatoric where there is an element of chance involved in the actual notes chosen). This rose up and ended on a chord of E major, ready for Paul's middle section.

Concept album: An album whose musical tracks share a common subject matter. Often the title and cover art also reflect the chosen theme, which could be a narrative or simply an idea.

Sgt Pepper's is often cited as the first **concept album**. It certainly began life this way. Paul McCartney's ideas for a storyline that followed a fictional band were abandoned after the first two tracks (although the reprise of the title track and the record sleeve help to maintain the album's unity) and the rest of the tracks have no particular connection. It is difficult to award the title of first concept album to a particular record, but important early examples are *Face to Face* (1966) by The Kinks, *Days of Future Passed* (1967) by The Moody Blues and *SF Sorrow* (1968) by the Pretty Things.

PSYCHEDELIC ROCK AND FOLK

As mentioned above, the psychedelic rock style preference was for longer tracks and therefore albums were more useful than singles. Psychedelic folk bands (bands that used more traditional folk instruments, included an element of acoustic music and followed the musical idioms associated with folk) tended to produce albums with tracks the length of commercial singles. On the next page is a list of the most successful albums in these two categories from the late 60s, where R stands for rock and F for folk.

Year	Artist	R/F	Album
1966	The Byrds	F	*Fifth Dimension*
	The Mamas and the Papas	R	*If You Can Believe Your Eyes and Ears*
1967	The Moody Blues	R	*Days of Future Passed*
	Pink Floyd	R	*The Piper at the Gates of Dawn*
	Jefferson Airplane	R	*Surrealist Pillow*
	Traffic	R	*Mr Fantasy*
	The Doors	R	*The Doors*
	Donovan	F	*Sunshine Superman*
1968	Grateful Dead	R	*Anthem of the Sun*
	The Pretty Things	R	*SF Sorrow*
	The Incredible String Band	F	*The Hangman's Beautiful Daughter*

The Rolling Stones produced the album *Aftermath* in 1966. This was notable on two counts: it was the first album with songs written exclusively by band members, and it used unusual instruments on a number of the tracks. However, it was still in their trademark Chicago electric blues style. The single released from the album, 'Paint It Black', for example, sees Brian Jones playing a sitar for a repeated riff that doubles the vocals and mimics Indian melodies with its **stepwise movement**, moving up the F minor scale to B♭ and down again to E♮.

Jones also plays Appalachian mountain dulcimers and African marimbas (large wooden xylophones) for various songs. The band's 1967 album *Their Satanic Majesties Request* was an imitation of *Sgt Pepper's*, but they were much more musically successful when they returned to their blues style with their next album, *Beggar's Banquet* (1968). The opening track, entitled 'Sympathy For The Devil', helped to reinforce their image as bad boys, and it was made the subject of an artistic film by the Franco-Swiss film director Jean Luc Godard, which included a substantial amount of fly-on-the-wall studio footage.

Blues styles can come under the wider description of psychedelic when they are more experimental in nature, for example the electric blues of Jimi Hendrix, and Eric Clapton's long improvisations with British supergroup Cream.

Stepwise movement: When consecutive notes go up or down by one step. Also called conjunct movement. When music jumps about it is known as disjunct.

JIMI HENDRIX EXPERIENCE, 'PURPLE HAZE' (1967)

Recorded on the album *Are You Experienced*, this track is one of his more psychedelic ones.

Jimi Hendrix

Transition: Musical passage used for connecting two other sections together, sometimes known as a bridge passage.

Hendrix is famous for his revolutionary electric guitar techniques, and the track begins with an introduction of two bars of guitar and bass playing together at the strange sounding interval of a diminished 5th (bass on E, guitar on B♭), followed by eight bars of distorted lead guitar playing melodic phrases beginning with:

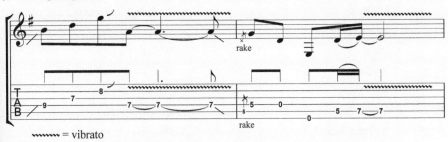

ᗺᗺᗺᗺ = vibrato

This introduction concludes with the two-bar chord pattern, played twice, that will be used for the song proper: E | G A :||

↓

0:32 The vocals enter with the song title, using a spacy sound processed with reverb and echo/delay, and running for eight bars ending with the unaccompanied line "scuse me while I kiss the sky'. This is picked up by a powerful octave line between guitar and bass.

↓

0:52 Verse 2 repeats the music although the ending is changed when a connecting passage of music to the words 'help me!' (**transition**) leads into a

↓

1:18 blues-based guitar solo, which includes some sitar-like lines.

↓

1:35 The introduction's guitar phrases are then repeated with 'oohs' and 'aahs' in the background, leading to:

↓

1:53 Verse 3.

↓

2:13 Then there follows a coda section of 17 bars that becomes increasingly complex and psychedelic with a high wailing guitar and spoken voices, followed by a fade-out.

Hendrix's guitar-playing has influenced many guitar players. He uses a wide range of techniques including hammer-ons and pull-offs (see p. 25), feedback, slides, string bends and double stops (two notes at once). He also uses harmonics, which is where the string is touched lightly at a particular point to produce a high, clear, flute-like sound. These points along the string (called nodes) include:

Point along the string	Note produced
Halfway	octave higher
Quarter of the way	two octaves higher
A third of the way	octave + 5th higher (e.g. E2 becomes B3)
A fifth of the way	two octaves + major 3rd (e.g. E2 becomes G♯4)

Jimi Hendrix was also fond of electronically processing his guitar sound (fx), often using portable pedals that could be switched with the foot.

These included:

Pedal type	Resulting effect
Fuzz face	Distorted sound as if the speaker is damaged
Wah wah	Sweeping the frequencies of a sound, resulting in a human-like cry or the uncovering of a trumpet bell
Chorus	A slight delay mixed with changing pitch ends up sounding as if there are multiple players
Univibe	Chorus-like effect that spins round like a Leslie speaker (see p. 42)
Octavia	Doubles notes in octaves
Phase	Sweeping sound created by splitting a signal (see p. 42)

He also would overdrive his amplifiers to produce distortion and set very high volume levels to produce feedback. On occasions he would play his guitar behind his back or with his teeth.

Tragically, Jimi Hendrix passed away in September 1970, but not before making some legendary appearances at pop music festivals in Monterey (1967) and Woodstock (1969) in the USA, and Woburn (1968) and the Isle of Wight (1970) in the UK. The last of these was attended by a record 500,000 people.

The Dallas Arbiter Fuzz Face effect pedal

Outdoor pop music festivals began in the 1960s but continue successfully to this day. In the UK the Glastonbury Festival has been going since 1970 and the world music festival WOMAD co-founded by Peter Gabriel since 1982.

The band Cream can be considered a psychedelic rock band. The cover for their second album *Disraeli Gears* (1967) certainly bears this out, with its colourful artwork. Only a few of the tracks can be thought of as demonstrating their blues roots, and many of them use highly psychedelic sounds. The band consisted of three expert performers: Eric Clapton, formally of The Yardbirds, was their lead guitarist, with Jack Bruce on bass and Ginger Baker on drums. Influenced by British blues performers such as Alexis Korner and John Mayall, the group began their work with covers of Delta and Chicago blues classics such as Robert Johnson's 'Crossroads' and Muddy Waters' 'Rollin' and Tumblin''. Their own songs featured heavy lead riffs and long instrumental improvisations. The octave lead and bass guitar riff of their 1968 hit single 'Sunshine Of Your Love' is worth quoting for its sheer power, as it drives the song along under the vocals. Note the tab positions showing how far up the fretboard Clapton is playing.

Cream

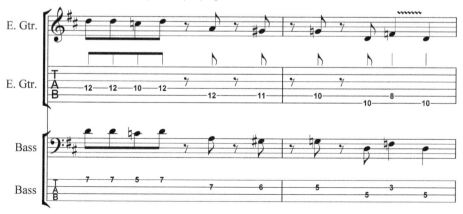

Finally for the psychedelic movement, Donovan, the folk singer from Scotland, deserves a mention. Like Dylan he was influenced by Woody Guthrie, as evidenced by his finger-picking acoustic guitar playing. His hits include 'Catch The Wind' and 'Colours' (both from 1965), 'Mellow Yellow' (1966) and 'Hurdy Gurdy Man' (1968). Donovan's easy going character helped him befriend many other musicians, including The Beatles, Joan Baez and Bruce Springstein, and he is still appearing in acoustic pop festivals well into the 21st century.

INFLUENCES FROM JAMAICA

A style of music grew up in the West Indies during the 1960s that would have a profound effect on all music to come. This was called ska, which by 1966 had developed into rocksteady and by the end of the decade into reggae.

In the 1960s, Jamaicans would listen to music radio broadcasts from the USA and the music records of military personnel stationed in bases on the island. They would put sound systems in vans and tour around various venues playing jump blues and R&B dance music. There would be a deejay for these shows called a 'toaster', who would call out dancers' names, tell jokes and make boastful comments all while the music was playing. His vocal delivery is seen as a precursor to **rap**.

Rap: Lyrics, usually rhyming, spoken in rhythm above a musical accompaniment.

Soon local record producers encouraged Jamaican talent to make their own music that both imitated the US styles they heard and added their own rhythms. The ska style was born. This was an up-tempo dance music featuring a heavy upstroke guitar on beats 2 and 4, a strong four-in-a-bar bass line, and brass instruments playing chordal interjections between phrases. Well-known bands included the Skatalites, produced by Prince Buster. A ska version of 'My Boy Lollipop' sung by Millie Small became an international hit in 1964.

As the same time as ska became popular, Jamaica gained independence from Britain (1962), but as music tastes changed in the USA so did the island's music. In 1966 the rocksteady genre was created, which is characterised by a more relaxed tempo while maintaining the offbeat guitar chords found in ska. Other characteristics of the style included what was known as the one-drop drum beat (a heavy bass drum and snare accent on the third beat), a heavy bass playing more syncopated rhythms than those found in ska and a reduced use of brass and saxes. The soulful R&B sounds of Stax Records in Memphis, and Afro-Cuban drumming techniques also influenced the musical language of rocksteady.

Analogue: Musical recording which uses a physical representation of the sound (for example, the grooves on a vinyl record copy the shape of the soundwave they are recording), as opposed to digital recording, which converts the sound into a series of binary (on/off) patterns.

By the late 1960s, bass lines had become particularly syncopated, with a clear melodic character, and tempi had slowed even more. The **analogue** delay sound processor had been imported into Jamaican studios and was applied to the offbeat guitar chords. Brass and saxes had almost gone and rhythm was all important. Rocksteady had transformed in reggae.

Black music in the form of Motown and soul continued to develop in the latter part of the decade. Hit records by Motown artists included Diana Ross and The Supremes ('You Can't Hurry Love', 1966) and Marvin Gaye ('I Heard It Through The Grapevine', 1968), and the soul singer Aretha Franklin had a number-one hit with 'Respect' (1967) for Atlantic Records. As the decade drew to a close, jazz, R&B and soul merged into a style that became known as funk, led by the pioneering and energetic singer James Brown.

DEVELOPMENTS IN MUSIC TECHNOLOGY

- There was a gradual move towards eight-track recording during the decade. In 1966 3M introduced their M23 – a one-inch-tape eight-track machine (the wider and faster-moving the tape, the higher the quality of sound) that became widely used in many top studios. In 1967 Ampex produced a prototype 16-track recorder. The Moody Blues were the first band to make use of the new eight-track machine at Decca Studios in 1968 with their album *In Search of the Lost Chord*.
- Mixing desks grew in size to match multi-tracking capability.
- ADT and flanging effects were invented at EMI studios, Abbey Road in 1966.
- Bands made extensive use of phase shifting as an effect (for example, The Small Faces, 'Itchycoo Park', 1967).
- In 1967 the Moog synthesiser became popular, and the first rock band recordings using the instrument appeared (The Doors, 'Strange Days'). Wendy Carlos released a groundbreaking album called *Switched-On Bach* in 1968, establishing the synthesiser as a serious instrument.
- Guitar amplifiers became more powerful and were overdriven to provide distortion. Foot-pedal distortion such as fuzz boxes were invented. Solid-state amplifiers were introduced (using transistors) resulting in cheaper, lighter and more reliable products, although many players still preferred the warmer sound of the old valve (vacuum tube) amps.

CHAPTER 4

The 1970s

BACKGROUND

The decade was one of technological innovation, combined with economic depression. Britain now had television in colour, and the clothes worn by fashion-conscious bands on the BBC chart show *Top of the Pops* appeared even more outrageous. Album sales became as important as singles, and the portable cassette could be used for listening to music on the go. The easy transfer of vinyl albums to cassette, a real worry for the music industry as it was possible to borrow a record from a friend and copy it without purchasing the original, simply helped to popularise bands that would not have been heard otherwise, especially in non-Western countries. Note: the situation today is similar with digital audio easily accessed from the internet and able to be copied in high quality with the right software, but often this simply helps publicise the music.

Many of the military personnel that returned home in the early 1970s after the Vietnam War were African Americans, who became disillusioned with their role in society. The assassination of the civil rights activist Martin Luther King (1968) had led the black population to adopt more radical views, which were manifested in the black power movement. The musical genre funk is often seen as embodying these struggles, and an illustration of this can be seen with Sly and the Family Stone's 'There's A Riot Goin' On' (1971).

Music in the 1970s became increasingly diverse, with bands building on the experiments of the late 1960s and taking the various stylistic elements further afield. Studio-conceived albums became even more of a norm, and some FM radio station programmes became dedicated to the long tracks. This was music to listen to and didn't belong in the dance hall. Soul styles, however, developed into funk and disco, folk and psychedelic styles persisted, and rock music split into the many different but related sub-genres listed on the next page.

Genre	Examples
Heavy (or hard) rock	Led Zeppelin, Deep Purple
Prog(ressive) rock	Pink Floyd, Genesis, Yes, ELP
Latin rock	Santana
Glam rock	David Bowie, Sweet, T.Rex, Queen
Soft rock	Elton John, Fleetwood Mac, 10cc, Billy Joel
Country rock	Eagles, Doobie Brothers, Emmylou Harris
Punk rock	The Clash, The Sex Pistols, The Damned, The Jam, The Ramones
New wave	Blondie, The Cars, Elvis Costello

DEVELOPMENTS IN ROCK MUSIC

While Led Zeppelin's first albums were released in 1969, continuing the tradition of Cream and The Yardbirds, their heavy blues rock style, which sometimes combined with elements of acoustic folk and synth-driven prog rock, belongs to the 1970s. Their four-man line-up consisted of Jimmy Page (guitar), John Paul Jones (bass and keyboards), Robert Plant (vocals) and John Bonham (drums). They continued producing albums throughout the decade, which they promoted by their extensive touring with stadium rock concerts, composing music that could be performed live rather than just using studio techniques. They did use some spacy effects on occasions, notably when Page would play his electric guitar with a violin bow, but were also completely at home performing with acoustic instruments. Their famous track 'Stairway To Heaven' (1971) begins acoustically with guitar and recorders, then an electric 12-string guitar is added with bass and drums, and finally the music breaks into heavy rock with electric lead guitar and wailing vocals. The lyrics of this song connect to the Eastern religious idea of spiritual enlightenment so beloved of the hippy movement.

MUSICAL EXAMPLE

LED ZEPPELIN, 'STAIRWAY TO HEAVEN' (1971)

The music begins gently with an acoustic steel guitar playing a four-bar picked solo that features a chromatically descending lower line.

00:12 This repeats with sustained recorder parts providing chords – added by overdubbing in the studio. In live performance the band's keyboard player John Paul Jones would use a Mellotron to create these sounds (see p. 43). Two more four-bar phrases extend this section, with the recorders gradually taking a more melodic role, and the harmony adopting a modal sound with the use of D major chords in A minor (transposed Dorian mode: see p. 29).

00:52 After an interrupted cadence with the harmony ending on chord VI (F major), Robert Plant's vocals enter with lyrics following the repeated four-bar phrasing for a total of five times.

2:00 The vocals drop out, and after one more instrumental version of the opening a fuller texture is used, with a 12-string guitar added to accompany the words 'Ooh – it makes me wonder'.

2:38 A second verse begins, but only lasts for two of the four-bar repeats, and the 'Ooh – it makes me wonder' continues the music before more lyrics for another verse and more instrumental music.

4:20 Drums enter with a medium rock rhythm, and a new melody vocal begins with a little more urgency.

5:07 The section repeats.

5:32 More powerful electric guitar semiquaver chords lead to an extended lead guitar solo.

6:44 A heavy rock section begins with more aggressive vocals, which eventually slows for a repeat of the title vocals.

The song is remarkable for the variety and musical interest that can be achieved from a basic four-bar harmonic pattern.

Deep Purple, another blues-based band from the UK, were interested in combining their music with classical styles, particularly the late Romantic concerto. At first they simply played their own music inserted next to classical pastiche – for example, 'Concerto For Group And Orchestra' (1970). Later they absorbed classical compositional devices such as sequence-based bravura into their playing. One Deep Purple track that adopts this approach is 'Highway Star' from the album *Machine Head* (1971) – an album that includes the well-known song 'Smoke On The Water'.

MUSICAL EXAMPLE

DEEP PURPLE, 'HIGHWAY STAR' (1970)

This driving track was important both for the fast pulse that was to inspire Motörhead and other 'speed metal' bands later in the 1970s and for the Baroque music figurations used during the organ and guitar solos between vocal verses.

The track begins with an eight-bar introduction, building tensions with the bass rising to a higher octave halfway through.

0:12 A second introductory passage begins after the music has settled down with a heavy **backbeat** snare, a guitar riff that emphasises the ♭VII note and an electrifying **glissando**, leading to a fast drum fill and two power chords of IV and ♭III.

0:34 The first verse vocals set off with 'Nobody gonna take my car I'm gonna race it to the ground'. The verse has an unusual construction: eight bars based around the key chord of G, with B♭ and C at the ends of phrases; four bars of F moving down in parallel chromatic chords to four of D; then six of A and four bars of adjacent chords in rhythmically anticipatory quavers, ending in a four-bar link to take us back for verse 2.

1:57 After verse 2 there is an extensive instrumental section beginning with guitar, but largely taken up by organ. This uses chromatic descending semiquaver **figurations** as in a Bach toccata.

2:53 A passage of syncopated riffs takes us back for

3:05 verse 3, which leads to

3:46 an extended guitar solo that uses sequences and figurations that wouldn't be out of place in a Vivaldi violin concerto (note: guitar 2 is a studio recorded layering and would be omitted in live performance):

Backbeat: Heavily stressed offbeats (accented beats 2 and 4). The word was famously used in the lyric 'It's got a backbeat, you can't lose it' from the Chuck Berry song 'Rock And Roll Music' (1957).

 Glissando: Sliding pitch.

Figurations: Patterns of notes.

Cadenza: Section of music where a soloist takes control of the tempo, playing music that is designed to display the performer's high level of skill.

5:05 The music returns to a repeat of verse 1 and crashes down to a coda full of **cadenza**-like improvisations from all the players and grinds to a halt.

Another band that ranks with Led Zeppelin and Deep Purple for heavy rock virtuosity is Black Sabbath. Their first album began with tolling church bells and a menacing guitar riff based on the diminished 5th: G down to C♯. This interval is called a tritone as it is made up of three whole tones; in medieval times it was banned and was known as 'the devil in music'. Their interest in Satanic subjects was copied later by bands such as Kiss and Slayer, and their 1970 album *Paranoid* has become a seminal album for the style.

PROG ROCK

The progressive (prog) rock style grew from the experimental and formal approaches of album tracks from the late 1960s. Bands such as Pink Floyd and Soft Machine took elements of psychedelia, avoided the more hippy aspects and injected a serious approach that became the hallmark of prog rock. It was a largely British style that appealed particularly to educated white middle-class males.

This style has a number of characteristics, although few of them are necessarily definitive. By its very nature it is diverse, experimental and varied. It is common to find:

- long tracks, with extended instrumental sections, including virtuoso soli
- complex lyrics, often with a dreamlike or visionary content
- intricate melodic lines and chromatic harmonies
- vocal harmonies
- electronic and classical instruments
- rhythmic variation, multiple time signatures and syncopation
- incorporation of other styles, such as jazz/world influences, and classical themes.

The musical language broke away from the blues, with vocal lines that avoided the decorations found in soul and instrumentation that brought keyboards up to an equal level of importance with guitars in both lead lines and accompaniment. Ideas were borrowed from classical music to control the longer tracks, with the **suite** being a favourite structure. Modern jazz harmonies and **avant-garde** techniques that used experimental textures and sounds from the physical environment can be traced in the music.

An early groundbreaking album from 1969 was *In the Court of the Crimson King* by King Crimson. The album used a variety of woodwind instruments and a Mellotron, and these instruments were given multiple layered overdubs on the eight-track machine at Wessex Studios in London.

Pink Floyd were already an experienced performing group when work began on *Dark Side of the Moon* in 1972. This was a concept album with the themes of madness, death, greed and alienation. Furthermore, the tracks merge into one another, employ numerous electronic and special effects, and yet produce a unified statement. The album was to advance the development of instrumental and recording studio techniques and confirm the band as imaginative composers on the world stage.

Suite: A collection of short pieces of music that have characteristics in common. These could be musical elements such as key, musical forms such as dance or simply where they originated, such as being taken from a stage show.

Avant-garde: Ultra-modern experimental styles.

Pink Floyd's Dark Side of the Moon *album cover*

MUSICAL EXAMPLE

PINK FLOYD, 'MONEY' (1973)

- The song begins with the sound of ringing cash registers, coins and torn paper which when looped produce an interesting rhythm.

0:11 The bass guitar enters playing a riff in $\frac{7}{4}$ time (with a feel of two bars of alternating $\frac{3}{4}$ and $\frac{4}{4}$ time signatures).

0:25 The drums and guitar enter, with the latter playing a B minor chord and using a fast echo repeat to continue the introduction. David Gilmour, the guitarist, used a Binson Echorec tape delay machine to produce this effect.

0:40 The vocals enter and sing 16 bars against the Bm/E harmonies (**transposed** Dorian mode), reaching a section where time signatures are further stretched to employ $\frac{5}{4}$ (in fact, 14 beats could be seen as two bars of $\frac{7}{4}$ but the vocal phrasing implies 3+5+3+3). More cash registers link to:

1:20 verse 2, which repeats the music of verse 1 and is followed by a substantial

2:01 tenor saxophone solo that employs a growling tone and **chorus effects**. This leads directly on to

3:04 a long heavily processed electric guitar solo in three sections. The middle uses a cleaner, quieter, less processed sound **hard panned** to the right and set to a beat with a more pronounced swing feel. The sections are divided by drum fills.

5:10 Verse 3 returns to music of verses 1 and 2.

5:42 The music fades out with echoed guitar chords and a wah-wah processor on a Wurlitzer electric piano, with various spoken comments.

Transposed: Moved to a different key.

Chorus effects: Applying slight delay and undulating pitch (frequency modulation) electronically to produce the impression that there are several people playing at once.

Hard panned: Sound is moved completely to the left or right speaker.

Money was not the only track on *Dark Side of the Moon* to have sounds from the real world spliced into the music. 'Time', for example, uses a whole collection of clocks, recorded in an antiques shop, producing a cacophony of chiming and alarms. The new 16-track machine installed in Abbey Road recording studio clearly inspired the band to use overdubbing to great effect.

Genesis had a long and successful run as a prog rock band. Their personnel has changed a number of times from 1969 to the present day, perhaps most significantly with their vocalist Peter Gabriel being replaced by the band's drummer Phil Collins in 1975. Their earlier albums contained some much longer tracks (*Nursery Crime*, 1971; *Foxtrot*, 1972, which features the 23-minute epic track 'Supper's Ready'). The band undertook world tours to promote their albums, which included elaborate light shows and stage effects. During the 1980s Phil Collins, in his career as a solo artist, became noted for his snare drum sound. This uses an effect known as a gated reverb, which is where the sound has large reverb effect applied to it, which as it fades is gated (cut off suddenly as it drops below a pre-defined level).

The band Yes included the classically trained keyboard virtuoso Rick Wakeman in their line-up, along with their high-register vocalist Jon Anderson, Chris Squire on bass and Steve Howe on guitar. Their style included psychedelic lyrics put across using powerful harmony vocals and complex musical arrangements. Wakeman joined the band for their fourth album (*Fragile*, 1971) which included a number of long tracks above eight minutes. Also from the album was the track 'Long Distance Runaround', which was only 3:30 and was released as the B-side to the hit single 'Roundabout' (which had to be edited to fit the single format).

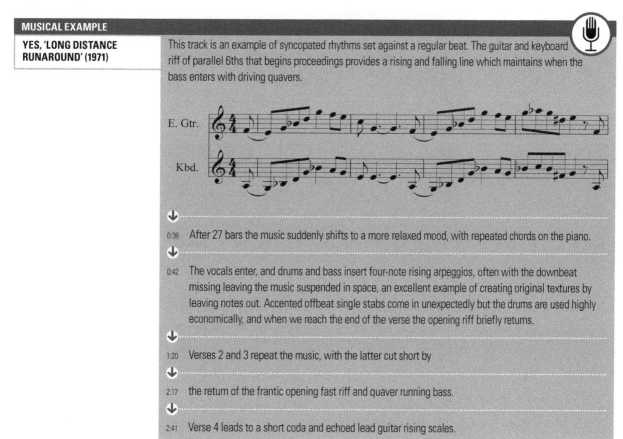

MUSICAL EXAMPLE

YES, 'LONG DISTANCE RUNAROUND' (1971)

This track is an example of syncopated rhythms set against a regular beat. The guitar and keyboard riff of parallel 6ths that begins proceedings provides a rising and falling line which maintains when the bass enters with driving quavers.

E. Gtr.

Kbd.

0:36   After 27 bars the music suddenly shifts to a more relaxed mood, with repeated chords on the piano.

0:42   The vocals enter, and drums and bass insert four-note rising arpeggios, often with the downbeat missing leaving the music suspended in space, an excellent example of creating original textures by leaving notes out. Accented offbeat single stabs come in unexpectedly but the drums are used highly economically, and when we reach the end of the verse the opening riff briefly returns.

1:20   Verses 2 and 3 repeat the music, with the latter cut short by

2:17   the return of the frantic opening fast riff and quaver running bass.

2:41   Verse 4 leads to a short coda and echoed lead guitar rising scales.

The band's sixth album *Tales from Topographic Oceans* was released in 1973. It was a double album with one music track per side, based on Eastern religious texts. The tracks were named 'Truth', 'Knowledge', 'Culture' and 'Freedom', but despite good commercial sales the album was criticised for pretentiousness. Rick Wakeman left the band after supporting it on a promotional tour of the album, for a successful solo career. Despite his love of the grand piano and the tape-based Mellotron he continued to build up his collection of keyboards as synthesiser technology developed.

MUSICAL INSTRUMENT

THE ANALOGUE SYNTHESISER

A synthesiser is an instrument that can create sounds electronically. Hammond organs are technically synthesisers which use a method called additive synthesis to create new sounds using drawbars by combining basic sine waves from the harmonic series – in other words, the sounds inherent in any natural vibrating object. Below are the natural overtones that are part of low C. These notes are not heard as pitches but rather as tone qualities or timbres of C, the sound's brightness related to their relative strength. The C is heard as the pitch because it is the most powerful, and in this case it is called the fundamental, with the other notes described as harmonics.

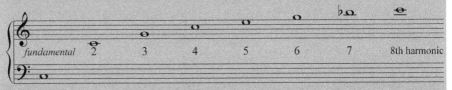

Analogue synthesisers use a system called subtractive synthesis whereby a rich waveform is produced by an oscillator (the electronic equivalent of a physical vibration) and then the harmonics are filtered out much the same as coffee grounds are filtered out leaving the drink (sound) we want.

An envelope (or sound shape) can be applied to the main components of a sound using three devices: the VCO (voltage controlled oscillator – providing the starting type of wave), the VCA (voltage controlled amplifier – setting how loud it is) and the VCF (voltage controlled filter – which affects the timbre). The envelope's shape is known as its ADSR (attack, decay, sustain and release), and different instruments have different envelope shapes. Here are some in terms of their loudness:

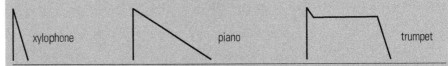

xylophone   piano   trumpet

Other parts of a sound can be set, such as vibrato (frequency modulation) or sliding between notes (portamento). The most obvious one in terms of sound is the choice of the starting waveform (VCO): for example, a sawtooth wave is used to create string sounds as it mimics the way a string slips many times from the sticky resin of the bow. Each of these settings was controlled individually using a dial, switch or slider, allowing the operator control over every aspect of a sound. A low frequency oscillator (LFO) is an electronic technique found in synthesisers where sound is subject to a slow change, either in pitch, producing vibrato in sound volume, producing a tremolo, or in filtering, producing a wah wah effect.

Early synthesisers were monophonic – in other words, they could only produce one note at a time. Famous among these was the Minimoog. It was used by many bands in the late 1960s and early 1970s because of its portability. Later polyphonic (many notes at once) and multi-timbral (many sounds at once) synthesisers were invented that had memory locations so that favourite settings could be accessed quickly without having to twiddle hundreds of dials and switches.

A popular analogue synthesiser of this type was the Prophet-5 made by Sequential Circuits in 1978. Vangelis used the top-of-the range Yamaha CS-80 for the soundtrack of the cult film *Blade Runner* (1982).

A Minimoog

LATIN ROCK

When the Latin-rock band Santana appeared at the Woodstock festival in 1969 they achieved immediate fame. Their first album (*Santana*), released soon after, became a worldwide hit, as did their follow-up album *Abraxas* (1970). Included on *Abraxas* were the hit singles 'Black Magic Woman' and 'Oye Como Va', a rock version of Tito Puente's cha cha cha/mambo-based 1963 composition. The band featured a large amount of Latin percussion instruments (congas, claves, bongos, maracas, and so on) as well as the standard rock instruments, including organ and the highly skilful electric guitar playing of the band's leader Carlos Santana. There would be long sections of improvisation, and vocals tended to be minimal. One famous track on *Abraxas* was the purely instrumental 'Samba Pa Ti'.

Congas

MUSICAL EXAMPLE	
SANTANA, 'SAMBA PA TI' (1970)	'Samba Pa Ti' begins with a relaxed lead guitar solo accompanied by gentle organ chords and congas. These tall Cuban drums are played with the hands using a variety of techniques:

- open sound – played with four fingers near the rim
- muted – again played near the rim but holding the fingers down
- bass tone – played with the full palm
- slap tone – cupping the hand and striking the drum hard.
- touch tone – can be used for rolls
- glissando – rubbing the third finger across the surface.

The verse is repeated (0:47) and then a Hammond organ lead break (1:32) introduces a bridge section, but the music moves seamlessly into double time (1:59) and we are left with a long lead guitar solo, that eventually dies away processed by spacy reverberation.

GLAM ROCK

The glam rock style takes its name from the outrageous clothes and costumes worn by bands at the time. These were highly colourful, glittering suits, high platform heel boots, make-up and spectacular hair styles. Performers adopted a sense of theatre often appearing somewhat camp or genderless. Chief among these artists was David Bowie and the bands T.Rex, Roxy Music, Slade, Mud and Sweet.

David Bowie as Ziggy Stardust

Bowie invented his first alter ego Ziggy Stardust in 1972, after the success of his single 'Space Oddity' (1969). It is impossible to pigeonhole this highly creative artist, and his classification as glam-rock artist was short lived. He had a hit single in the USA, co-written by John Lennon, called 'Fame' (1975) and continued to have hits during later decades, all based on theatrical themes or artsy subjects.

T.Rex was led by the singer Marc Bolan, and he is credited with starting off glam rock with his 1971 appearance on *Top of the Pops*. The band Sweet had 13 top-twenty hits in the UK during the 70s, including the number-one single 'Block Buster' (1973). This narrative track was also featured on *Top of the Pops* and is notable for the police siren that begins the music and sets the storyline. A heavy, dotted-rhythm, shuffle-like beat pounds away, and the spoken lyrics 'We just haven't got a clue what to do' are enhanced on the TV programme by the producer's kaleidoscopic visual tricks.

Roxy Music, led by Brian Ferry, were influenced by the fact that its principal members all came from art college. Partly because of this they maintained a carefully crafted image that applied not only to their stage performances but also to album covers, videos and promotional materials. They employed some unusual instruments, including the oboe, and the composer and synth player Brian Eno was among their membership for a time.

Other artists incorporated elements of glam rock into their stage acts. For example, Queen's third album *Sheer Heart Attack* (1974) included the hit single 'Killer Queen', which when performed on TV showed the band's glam rock inclinations, and the influence of lead singer Freddy Mercury's art college background. The band demonstrated a number of their trademarks in this song, with powerful close vocal harmonies for the title lyrics, $\frac{2}{4}$ bars to increase excitement at the ends of phrases, and superb guitar soloing from Brian May. The electronic phasing on the words 'Dynamite with a laser beam' betrayed their psychedelic influences. Their earlier album *Queen II* (1974) showed prog rock instrumental virtuosity, some heavy rock idioms and long tracks (such as 'March Of The Black Queen': six minutes) with fantasy-based lyrics. Another hugely successful track, taken from their fourth album (*A Night at the Opera*, 1975), was the operatically styled 'Bohemian Rhapsody', which to date is the third bestselling single of all time in the UK (after Elton John's 1997 'Candle In The Wind' and Band Aid's 1984/5 'Do They Know Its Christmas?').

MUSICAL EXAMPLE

QUEEN, 'BOHEMIAN RHAPSODY' (1975)

Queen album cover

'Bohemian Rhapsody' divides roughly into three sections, which in turn can be further broken down.

1. Ballad section:

An a cappella four-part vocal (sometimes processed by phasing and panning)

0:14   Close harmony singing is joined by the piano.

0:48   Freddie Mercury, the lead vocalist, plays piano to introduce his solo vocal verse 1, with his left hand crossing over his right for some high notes.

1:19   During the last bar of eight the drums enter with a cymbal roll, settling to a slow rock rhythm.

1:55   Verse 2 of the vocals continues the music, harmony vocals entering near its end, leading to

2:35   a lead guitar solo, using mostly scalic patterns.

2. 'Operatic' section:

3:02   The song moves into a faster tempo, beginning with repeated light piano chords.

A variety of vocal textures are employed to continue the music, including antiphonal (answering) phrases, heavy phrases with everyone emphasising the lyrics ('thunderbolts and lightning'), solo snippets from individual voices ('Galileo'), cascading **imitative entries** ('magnifico'), and more solos and answering phrases.

3:36   Harmony vocals continue with repeated vocal chords of 'Let me go' (3:46) panned across the speakers.

3:58   The section concludes with a **tutti**, everyone singing about the devil, and leads, with a chord V emphasis, to the next section.

3. Heavy rock section:

4:08   Led by a heavy rising electric guitar riff.

4:15   Vocals enter with offbeat chords stressing the ends of phrases.

4:36   Another rising lead and bass guitar riff leads to a slower section.

5:12   A return of the ballad music from the start concludes the structure and the sound of a **tam tam** note is left to die away.

The song was played on British TV using a groundbreaking promotional video, a practice that was to become increasingly common not just with studio-produced songs difficult to perform live, but also to get across a band's image or message.

Imitative entries: When musical lines are copied in different parts, appearing one after another.

Tutti: All performers playing or singing together.

Tam tam: Large metal gong.

Queen went on to become one of the most successful bands of the 1970s and 80s, until Freddie Mercury's untimely death in 1991, touring their music to vast audiences. Along with Led Zeppelin and The Rolling Stones they contributed to the subgenre of arena, or stadium rock, which featured huge stage productions to massive numbers, made possible by developments in amplification equipment and projection techniques.

SINGER-SONGWRITERS

Elton John was a singer-songwriter and pianist who managed to enhance the communication with his audience, and therefore his music, by adopting glittery suits and wildly exaggerated spectacle frames. Without the ability to dance around like a guitar player, being stuck at the piano, he cultivated a TV persona that encouraged camera operators to move around him instead.

Elton John had a gift for pop melody, and there is smooth tunefulness running through the slower tracks of his second album (*Elton John*, 1970). Many of these ballads use a favourite texture of John's copied by many other artists: arpeggiated piano chords with orchestral strings playing sustained chords underneath (known as a string 'pad'). Sometimes he would be more adventurous with string arrangements, almost symphonic, such as during the introduction and interlude section for 'Sixty Years On' (1970) or 'Funeral For A Friend', the opening track of his following album, *Goodbye Yellow Brick Road* (1973). His sweet soulful voice is equally at home with the up-tempo rocky numbers as it is with the ballads.

Elton John

MUSICAL EXAMPLE

ELTON JOHN, 'YOUR SONG' (1970)

'Your Song' is the opening track of the album *Elton John*, and is a relaxed love song in $\frac{4}{4}$ time with a semiquaver feel in the warm key of E♭ major.

Tonic pedal: Tonic refers to the first note of the key scale and a pedal is where a single note (usually in the bass, but not always) sustains while harmonies chage over or around it.

Straight away Elton John sets up rising and falling broken chords on the piano over a **tonic pedal** in the bass.

0:07 The vocals come in with the melody based around G, while changing harmonies move to create interesting chords such as the major 7th on IV (A♭maj⁷). The verse runs for eight bars of slow four time, with an additional half bar to take us back for verse 2, helping the relaxed mood by extending the normal verse length, yet not overdoing things with a whole extra bar.

0:38 Although the music for verse 2 is a repeat of verse 1, this time a lush string pad fills out the texture.

1:10 A middle section then begins, with the melody built at first on a repeated two-bar phrase, but then repeated half-bars that emphasise the words 'I hope you don't mind'. These build up to a pause of four seconds that hold the string chord, as though holding the breath. The tension then breaks as the melody falls downwards for 'How wonderful life is while you're in the world'.

1:44 The intro repeats and leads to verse 3 and 4, this time with an even fuller orchestration adding flowing acoustic guitar figures.

2:55 The middle section then repeats, leading to a coda that repeats the last four bars, and the song concludes with a satisfying repeat of the intro.

COUNTRY ROCK

Similarly relaxed styles can be found in the US folk and country rock genres of the time. James Taylor was well known on both sides of the Atlantic, and his albums from the late 1960s and early 1970s demonstrate a consummate skill as a singer-songwriter and finger-picking guitarist. He had a major breakthrough in 1970 with the single 'Fire And Rain', and he cultivated a theme of the impoverished country hobo on the road. His cover version of Carole King's 'You've Got A Friend' (1971) features overdubbed vocal harmonies in parallel 7ths; normally these would be discords, but in this context they manage to sound very sweet.

The Eagles – a country rock band

The Canadian folk singer Joni Mitchell also produced many folk guitar compositions, but as the decade progressed blended in jazz and rock influences. Neil Young's albums *After The Goldrush* (1970) and *Harvest* (1972) were similarly successful. Bob Dylan's backing group The Band had success with a number of country rock albums.

The Eagles were a country rock band that became global superstars. Hits such as 'Take It Easy' (1972), 'Desperado' (1973) and 'One Of These Nights' (1975) gained them a reputation as cowboy songsters worldwide. The title track to the album *Hotel California* (1976) features twanging 12-string guitars, electric and acoustic guitars, bass, drums, and backing vocals which use the Eagles' particular skill of producing interesting vocal harmonies and textures. It includes an impressive electric guitar solo quite different from the standard blues/rock guitarists' style, with heart-wrenching string bends and a climatic section of falling arpeggio patterns played by two members of the band:

MOTOWN AND FUNK

Motown records had continued success throughout the decade. Marvin Gaye broke new ground with his album *What's Goin' On* (1971), which concentrated on urban decay and military oppression. Although the Motown house band the Funk Brothers were used on the album, Gaye produced most of the tracks himself, setting a new trend at the label. Major artists such as Stevie Wonder composed important innovative albums, such as *Talking*

Book (1972), which contained the hit singles 'Superstition' and 'You Are The Sunshine Of My Life', and the double album *Songs in the Key of Life* (1976).

Despite the general trend towards music for listening, black music in the USA had continued the dance tradition of earlier decades. The exciting performer James Brown had combined gospel, soul and jazz to pioneer a new genre that became known as funk. This featured highly sophisticated rhythms and an urgent beat that was known as the 'groove', although tempi were slower than one would expect, commonly 80–100bpm. Riff-based songs were common, with horn stabs and a general staccato feel, the sound often being defined by what was left out rather than what was put in.

Bands that could be described as funk orientated included The Meters; Earth, Wind and Fire; and the producer and singer-songwriter George Clinton's collective Parliament Funkadelic, which used synthesisers and studio effects while maintaining a jazz-based live sound. Isaac Hayes became famous for his funk instrumental that was the basis of the soundtrack for the film *Shaft* (1971), and the style influenced artists as diverse as the Jackson 5, the jazz trumpeter Miles Davis and the fusion band Weather Report. The genre came to represent the black community and its stereotypes of coolness and gangster chic.

Counterpoint: Music that combines two or more melodic lines in such a way that they retain their independence. The adjective from the word counterpoint is 'contrapuntal'. Contrapuntal musical lines derive from shared harmonic progressions while employing different rhythms, while the related term 'polyphony' refers to melodic lines where the harmony is incidental. The great era of counterpoint is considered to be the Baroque period (1600–1750).

MUSICAL EXAMPLE

EARTH, WIND AND FIRE, 'SHINING STAR' (1975)

This song is considered a good example of funk music that has met mainstream success, achieving the number-one spot in both the R&B and pop charts in 1975. It has a big sound with brass, synthesisers, guitars and backing vocals.

Groove: the driving rhythmic feel of music that makes the listener want to get up and dance.

The music begins with two electric guitar playing in **counterpoint**, joined after four bars by a walking-bass guitar line.

0:10   A powerful high brass chord sets off a rhythmic **groove** based on the hard-hitting discordant sound of an $E^{7\sharp 9}$ chord (which combines a $G\sharp$ and $G\natural$).

0:13   When the vocals come in, several members come in ahead of the verse with 'yeah's and 'hey's, setting a party atmosphere. The lyrics of the verse refer to the the sentimental Disney ballad sung at the start of the animated film *Pinocchio* (1940), but soon turn away from these to go their own way.

The bass line moves around with complex syncopations and high vibrato notes, while the rhythm guitar maintains a repeated rhythmic drive with a heavy kick drum on beats 1 and 3 and snare/claps on beats 2 and 4. Brass interject with staccato stabs.

0:46   Vocals combine in harmonies and move up to high falsetto octaves. After 12 bars of the same harmony, the stability is broken as the music moves to a series of jazz-influenced chords – $A^7 D^9$ | $G^{13} C^9$ | to accompany the title lyrics.

0:56   At this point there is a fast-moving electric piano riff:

1:00   This is followed by a strong lead guitar solo, which is accompanied by rising parallel harmonies, taking the listener 'up to the sky' chromatically.

1:12   The verse and chorus repeat leading to a coda that maintains the groove with trumpet solos until we are left with a cappella vocals.

DISCO

In the middle of the decade a craze for dance clubs sprang up in Europe and the USA. Night clubs had normally featured live bands, but clubs playing records of the new style of funky dance pop became more common with DJs (disc jockeys) taking over the evening's entertainment. The clubs that played this music were known as discothèques, and so the style became known as disco. Spurred on by the success of the film *Saturday Night Fever*, starring John Travolta and featuring music by the Bee Gees ('Stayin' Alive' and 'Night Fever', 1978), clubs continued to increase in number, the male macho image in the film helping to counter the prejudice generally associated with the underground gay nightclub dance scene.

MUSICAL EXAMPLE	
THE BEE GEES, 'NIGHT FEVER' (1978)	The sound of a solo wah-wah guitar begins the track, but is immediately incorporated into a full sound with bass and high synth strings, combining with funky synthesiser rhythms and underpinned throughout with the disco four-on-the-floor kick drum.
	0:17 The penetrating high voice of Barry Gibb enters with the first verse. After eight bars
	0:36 the mood changes for six bars as the other two Gibb brothers (Robin and then Maurice) join in the vocals, with electric piano licks and glissandi adding colour, leading to
	0:48 a key change for the chorus, sung in octaves with a repeated series of seventh chords: C#m^7 I F#m^7 I Emaj^7 I F#m^7 :II and sustained high synth strings.
	1:06 The music settles on F# and this bridge gradually builds over eight bars with the harmonic rhythm (speed of chord change) increasing, leading up to
	1:24 a repeat of the chorus,
	1:40 a second verse,
	2:12 another chorus and a bridge.
	2:47 A repeated chorus leads to a fade-out.

MUSICAL EXAMPLE

GLORIA GAYNOR, 'I WILL SURVIVE' (1978)

A rising and falling piano arpeggio of $E^{7\sharp 9}$ holds the tension.

0:06   Gloria Gaynor begins the vocals in an out-of-tempo **colla voce** style, with chord changes on the first beat of the bar following the delivery of her phrasing.

0:23   A regular beat of 116bpm sets off the music with the usual four-on-the-floor disco kick drum, and the verse repeats three times for a total of 24 bars leading to

1:12   an instrumental of eight bars launched by a harp glissando, and featuring a string section lead that combines decoration (mordents and trills) with high sustained notes and semiquaver passages.

1:29   Four more verses follow (although the last could be thought of as a chorus with its emphasis on the title lyrics and its added string counter-melody).

2:34   The beat stops momentarily for a held pause. On the dance floor this would be eagerly anticipated, producing enjoyment as the regular tempo is resumed with two more verses.

3:12   Tenor sax solo.

3:28   Four more verses.

4:35   The tenor sax leads a fade-out.

The eight-bar harmony repeats throughout and follows a cycle of 5ths (see p. 9), and the dancers and listeners derive pleasure from the expected harmonic progression.

Variety is achieved through varying the orchestrations and excitement through Gaynor's powerful vocals combined with the constant driving pulse.

__Colla voce__: Italian for 'with the voice', this is an instruction to players to go with whatever tempo or phrasing the singer chooses.

Hook: The part of a song that is highly memorable and helps with its sales potential. A hook can be anything from an unusual twist in the melody of a chorus to a recurring rhythmic motif or some novel harmonies.

Polyrhythms: The simultaneous sounding of two or more independent rhythms, such as triplets against duplets, creating a complex pattern.

As far back as 1975 Gloria Gaynor had produced an album of dance music that merged the songs into a continuous long track, helping the job of the DJ, and in the same year Van McCoy's instrumental 'The Hustle' typified the new disco style, with a catchy **hook** above a regular, strong beat. The disco style had the following characteristics:

- Drummers would support the beat with four crotchet beats in a bar on the kick drum (known as four on the floor) and driving semiquavers on closed high hats. Latin-derived **polyrhythms** can also be found.
- Bass players reinforced the regular beat with repeated patterns often involving octave leaps.
- Vocalists used high soaring melodies with reverberation.

- Producers included high orchestral strings, horns and synthesisers, sometimes playing in unison.

Towards the end of the decade disco became popular in Europe, although music here was less funk-influenced. The Italian record producer Giorgio Moroder worked with the US singer Donna Summer to produce a revolutionary disco sound in 1977, one that included a wholly synthesised backing track. 'I Feel Love' used sequenced arpeggios and ostinato bass lines in a solid regular rhythmic loop, high over which Donna Summer sang a hypnotic melody of long notes.

The bass ostinato pattern was:

which moved up and down as the harmonies changed, while Summer's vocals descended by step to the words 'I feel love'.

The sounds were created on a Moog modular synthesiser system and the backing was one of the earliest to use an electronic **sync track**, recorded on track 16 of a Studer multi-track, which locked all the overdubs together to produce a very tight beat.

Europop was a particularly manufactured sounding disco style that limited its international influence to a few highly successful bands. Boney M was based in Germany and had a Jamaican influence. The band's biggest hit was the double A-side 'Rivers Of Babylon'/'Brown Girl In The Ring' (1978). The Swedish group Abba, which consisted of two couples, won the Eurovision Song Contest with 'Waterloo' (1974), going on to have a string of number-one hits, eight in the UK and one in the USA ('Dancing Queen', 1976). Their style employed sweeping melodies, often sung in close harmony, with glossy production values and a glittery stage presentation.

Disco had its roots in all pop music genres, including Motown (Diana Ross), soul (Barry White), jazz (KC and the Sunshine Band) and even classical (Walter Murphy's hit 'A Fifth Of Beethoven', 1976, was a disco version of Beethoven's Symphony No. 5).

REGGAE

Another black music style that developed in the 1970s, reggae had emerged in Jamaica from its predecessors ska and rocksteady, and was performed at a slower tempo with a more laid-back feel. The bass guitar and the percussion are brought to the foreground, and guitar and keyboards sent back in the mix, thus exchanging the traditional roles of these instruments.

- A reggae bass line is very melodic and is often the defining feature of a track. It normally avoids the first beat of the bar altogether and is made up of short phrases moving in quavers or repeated semiquavers. It complements the percussion section in terms of setting up a groove.
- A standard drum kit is used, with the snare tuned very high or turned off completely to make the drum sound like timbales, and rim shots and tom tom notes are common.

Sync track: A signal is recorded to one track of a multi-track tape recorder – usually an outside one, such as the first or last, to cut down leakage onto other tracks – and then other music will only play when it receives the playback signal. This simple syncronisation used a square wave signal in the early days, but later more sophisticated systems were employed – such as SMPTE, where locked tracks could even be rewound or forwarded and memory locations could be added.

Drums also avoid beat 1, preferring to stress beat 3.

- The guitar mostly plays chords on the offbeat, beats 2 and 4, with short damped upstrokes.
- Piano and organ also play on the offbeat, although the organ adds extra quaver chords and sometimes melodic runs.
- Horns sometimes play **countermelodies** and would normally be made up of sax, trumpet and trombone.

Island Records was founded in Jamaica by Chris Blackwell, but relocated to London in 1959. It specialised in bringing recordings from the island and releasing them in the UK, to meet a demand from the many West Indian immigrants in the UK keen to hear music from home. In 1972 Blackwell signed the band Bob Marley and the Wailers, who became the defining sound of roots reggae for the rest of the decade. The roots reggae style incorporated elements of the Rastafarian religion into the lyrics, with a political message concerning the plight of the underprivileged Jamaican.

Marley had hits with 'No Woman No Cry' (1974) and 'One Love' (1977). Eric Clapton produced a cover version of Marley's song 'I Shot The Sheriff' (1974), which was a big hit, and inspired many listeners to look up Bob Marley's music.

A subgenre of reggae is dub. This originated when Jamaican producers would strip the vocals from an existing recording and then emphasise the drum and bass parts (ending up with what was known as the 'riddim'). Next they would add extensive echo and/or reverb effects. Sometimes natural sounds or new instruments would also be added, and the result would provide a background for live toasters (see p. 48) to talk over.

Countermelodies: Melodies that run at the same time as the main tune. Sometimes known as a descant when applied to a countermelody running *above* a main tune in a hymn.

Bob Marley

PUNK ROCK

Punk rock was a reaction to the perceived excesses of prog and glam rock and to the mind-altering approach of psychedelia. It began in the middle of the decade and was a back-to-basics movement that preferred performance to studio work and avoided expensive equipment.

The punk rock musical genre grew out of a wider phenomenon that spread across US and British society during the 1970s. Its beginnings can be traced to groups known a garage bands in the USA, where young musicians adopted a home-produced approach. The style of proto-punk artists such as Iggy Pop was to lead directly to the first punk bands in the mid-1970s, the most important of which was the Ramones. Their music was known for its direct communication, generally using fast tempi and basic harmonies and avoiding the long guitar solos of mainstream rock music, which they considered over the top. Punk musicians reacted against what they saw as the self-indulgent excesses of prog rock – the intellectual approach of long musical forms, over-produced studio albums and especially the displays of instrumental virtuosity. In addition, they disliked the commercial sound and hedonistic styles of disco music.

In Britain there was general dissatisfaction with the declining state of the economy and the way government was dealing with it. The music business was seen as middle class

Punk fashion

and its products as overinflated. Punks thought that music should be for the masses and playable by unskilled performers who had a message to get across.

The new style avoided the use of keyboards and fancy production techniques, and the basic line-up of guitars, bass and drums became the norm. Vocals were shouted, spoken or at least muttered, and used overtly political lyrics. The music used a limited range of chords, with the bass playing repeated root notes and the drums avoiding any syncopations. Frantically fast tempi were adopted, and guitars were played very loudly with heavy distortion. UK bands included the Sex Pistols ('Anarchy In The UK', 1976, which begins with the lyrics 'I am an anti-Christ'), The Clash ('White Riot', 1977, based on racial issues) and The Damned ('Smash It Up', 1979).

Non-functional harmony: Chord series that do not follow the traditional rules of harmonic progression: for example, IV I II I V I I is functional, whereas II I VII I IV I III is not.

Sus⁴: Chords using the suspended fourth. For example, Csus⁴ is C–F–G, where in traditional harmony the F is carried from the chord before and moves down to an E in the following chord to 'resolve'. Modern styles treat the chord as an entity, not worrying about the chords either side.

MUSICAL EXAMPLE

THE DAMNED, 'SMASH IT UP' (1979)

The song is highly direct in its message, and the vocals are clear and strongly supported by the constant driving rhythm.

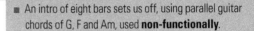

- An intro of eight bars sets us off, using parallel guitar chords of G, F and Am, used **non-functionally**.

0:11 The lyrics of the verse dictate the irregular phrase lengths so that we end up with two bars of $\frac{4}{4}$ and two bars of $\frac{6}{4}$, repeated.

0:26 The chorus begins with the parallel chords used in the intro; the lyrics 'Smash it up' are chanted in unison by the singers.

0:37 Verse 2 repeats the music of verse 1.

0:52 A second chorus follows.

1:03 A strange link section begins where one would normally expect an instrumental solo, but although the drums keep the beat going the guitars collapse in confusion after some **sus⁴** chords and a repeated high note that might have been the start of a solo.

1:16 There is now a complete change, with the chord of E and low repeats of the title lyrics.

1:27 A genuine guitar solo follows, over the chord of F♯.

1:38 A bridge section based on B major harmonies leads us to

1:50 verse 3 then to

2:06 the third chorus and a

2:17 link to a coda, where even the tempo falls apart.

The song is deceptive in that its use of parallel harmonies and irregular phrases seem naïve but in fact work very well, producing a hard-hitting song that was initially banned by the BBC.

NEW WAVE

Punk ideology was adopted by the art-school music scene and a style of music called new wave was born. This maintained the back-to-basics approach but injected some sophisticated lyrics, turning punk's anger to cynicism. Blondie ('Heart Of Glass', 1979) and Talking Heads were bands using this style. The arrival of MTV in 1981 would usher in new wave's most important period.

The US band Blondie made a considerable contribution at the end of the decade. They were firmly rooted in the post-punk/new-wave style, but their instrumentation looked forward to the synthpop genre of the 1980s, although they did not adopt the minimalist approach to band membership that this particularly British style was to feature.

MUSICAL EXAMPLE	
BLONDIE, 'HEART OF GLASS' **(1979)**	In this track Blondie introduced elements of disco by having a drum machine control much of the music. A Roland CR-78 drum machine pattern was recorded on one track of the 24-track tape recorder. The drummer then recorded just his bass drum on another track, keeping it exactly in time, playing four-on-the-floor crotchets. Next the rest of the kit was overdubbed.

The bass line was partly provided by a SH-1000 synth where, the player held down the bass harmony note and repeated semiquaver notes were produced locked to the control voltage signal being sent from the drum machine. A bass guitar was also recorded on another track.

Another synth player on a Polymoog produced sweeping chords.

Several guitar tracks were added, including one with a timed tape delay to match the synth signal's rhythm.

Debbie Harry, the band's lead singer, whose hair colour gave the group their name, was recorded on two tracks, double-tracking the vocals to produce her unique sound, and on occasions recording an additional alto line an octave lower. Male vocals were used in the outro.

Along with all this technical innovation the music itself is highly memorable. Three particular moments deserve a mention:

- The first notes of the vocals (0:16) are five repeated 6ths above the key-chord root, transforming the E harmony into E^6 and making the singer's entry more powerful.

- The unusual harmonic progression of I I IIImaj I IIImin I I is part of the main hook (E I C♯ I C♯m I E I).

- When the middle vocal section returns as an instrumental (1:58) the phrase lengths are shortened by a beat, making alternating $\frac{3}{4}$ and $\frac{4}{4}$ bars and helping to move the music on. This would not affect anyone dancing to the music, who would be moving to the solid crotchet beats no matter how many there were in a bar.

Other post-punk bands at the end of the decade sought more complex textures and experimental approaches typified by bands such as Siouxsie and the Banshees ('Hong Kong Garden', 1978). The successful pub rock scene that grew up in the mid-70s particularly in London gave rise to artists such as Elvis Costello and The Attractions ('Watching the Detectives', 1977) and Ian Dury and The Blockheads ('Hit Me With Your Rhythm Stick', 1979) – bands that led eventually to the indie scene of future decades.

DEVELOPMENTS IN MUSIC TECHNOLOGY

- Polyphonic synthesisers became more common and were adopted by many bands (Prophet-5, Yamaha GX1, Korg PS-3100).
- The vocoder, a specialised speech synth effect, was pioneered by the German electronic band Kraftwerk in 1972.
- The Technics SL-1200 was brought out, the standard turntable for DJs.
- In 1976, the VHS video format was introduced in Japan.
- In 1977, the Roland Corporation released the MC-8 Microcomposer, the first microprocessor-based digital sequencer.
- Roland CR-78 programmable drum machine was introduced (used by Blondie on their single 'Heart Of Glass').
- In 1979, the Fairlight CMI digital sampler was invented.
- Also in 1979, the Sony Walkman personal cassette player was launched.

CHAPTER 5

The 1980s

BACKGROUND

At the start of the decade there was a swing to the political right in both the USA, with a newly elected Republican government under Ronald Reagan, and in the UK, when the Conservative Party led by Margaret Thatcher won the 1979 general election. The punk movement of the late 1970s, partially born out young people's discontentment with the way society was developing, did not fit with the new mood of the country. Music, among other products, needed to become more marketable, and although the excesses of punk rock had been somewhat toned down by new wave bands, further steps in this direction were required. The aggressive approach to musical performance still lingered, but now a band's image became more important, with a focus on fashion and individualism as well as the music itself.

SYNTHPOP

In the UK, the innovative singer and composer Gary Numan had a number of hits in 1979 that featured synthesisers (e.g. 'Are Friends Electric?' and 'Cars'). It was the beginning of a new style of music that became known as synthpop.

Influences from Germany can be traced in the style, with progressive electronic band Tangerine Dream and the more pop-orientated group Kraftwerk (*The Man-Machine*, 1978) being an inspiration to many of the new bands.

Kraftwerk album cover

There had been significant developments in synthesiser technology, and musicians found their ideas much easier to realise. For example, synthesisers themselves became more portable, with memory locations to store favourite 'patches' and commercially available 'banks' of new sounds that could be 'loaded' into the instruments. Furthermore, in 1982 a group of manufacturers decided to furnish their products with a common protocol for communication between devices, called MIDI (Musical Instrument Digital Interface). This meant that instruments could be connected together to transfer

Note-off and note-on events: Terms used to describe when a note on a keyboard is depressed and released. The events register the beginning and ending of sounds using the digital protocol known as MIDI.

Ostinato: Repeated pattern of notes on the same instrument at the same pitch.

Although the Synclavier II used sound creation technology, it was not an analogue synth as such. It was a hybrid system that used a computer, digital synthesis and sampling to create its sound.

information, including **note-off and note-on events**, enabling sound layering and timing clocks controlled by pre-programmable sequencers. At first sequencers were manufactured in hardware form. The so-called step sequencers would use a grid, usually of 16 divisions to represent semiquavers in a $\frac{4}{4}$ bar and composers would set up the pitches that would play at different timing positions. The end result was a bar of music that looped round, producing an **ostinato**. The sequencers could produce several bars that would be connected end to end and thus a whole song could be produced. A similar technique was used for rhythm patterns and so the programmable drum machine became part of the ensemble.

Later software computer programs were used to produce more sophisticated sequences. The Atari ST was the computer of choice as it featured built-in MIDI sockets, but the Commodore 64 was also popular.

In 1981 the duo Soft Cell, made up of Marc Almond (vocals) and Dave Ball (instruments) had an international hit with 'Tainted Love', a cover of the song popular in northern soul clubs such as Va Va's in Bolton and Wigan Casino in the 1970s, but recorded originally by the US singer Gloria Jones in 1965. It was from their album *Non-Stop Erotic Cabaret* and had an accompaniment of just synthesisers.

MUSICAL EXAMPLE

SOFT CELL, 'TAINTED LOVE' (1981)

Dave Ball used a variety of synthesisers on this early synthpop classic, including a bass synthesiser for the main riff – a Korg Synthe-Bass SB-100 – a Synclavier for the opening two high 'blink, blink' crotchets that appear every two bars at the beginning, and a Roland TR-808 drum machine.

Marc Almond from Soft Cell

The song begins with an introduction. It lasts for eight bars and features the 'blink, blink' sound every two bars, with the only other instrument being the TR-808 simply playing alternative bass and snare crotchet beats. After four bars, a triplet fill leads into

0:06   a bass synth riff.

0:11   The bass continues under the vocal line, a characteristic of which is the syncopation that results from the 'blink, blink' notes that continue to appear at the start of every two bars.

The verse runs for 16 bars (eight lots of two) and leads to

0:39   a ten-bar bridge that is really eight bars extended by two. These are used to create emphasis on the V note leading to

0:56   a high note on the word 'All', which falls down in a glissando slide to begin a chorus based on the song title, with backing vocals between phrases. This chorus is short-lived and takes us back for

1:03   a second verse of ten bars

1:29   a second bridge and

1:46   chorus material that is extended in a semi-improvised vocal emphasising 'tainted love' and a fade-out. The song maintains its four-in-a-bar beat throughout and is eminently danceable, as is much of the synthpop genre.

Highly successful synthpop bands of the 1980s included Ultravox, Human League and Depeche Mode. The duo format became common as synthesisers and sequencers made it unnecessary to use large numbers of musicians, such as horn players. Some successful synthpop duos are listed below with a hit single for each:

Band	Single	Year
OMD (Orchestral Manoeuvres in the Dark)	'Souvenir'	1981
Yazoo	'Only You'	1982
Eurythmics	'Sweet Dreams (Are Made Of This)'	1983
Pet Shop Boys	'West End Girls'	1984
Erasure	'Sometimes'	1986

The music of many of the synthpop groups would feature long passages of sequenced loops. The Pet Shop Boys, for example, used the expensive Fairlight CMI computer-controlled sampler to produce these looping sequenced patterns on their hit single 'It's A Sin' (1987), along with choral chanting and claps of thunder, whereas Alison Moyet used the more affordable **Roland MC-4** hardware sequencer on many of the tracks of her album *Alf* (1984) after leaving Yazoo for a solo career (listen to the opening of the second track, 'Honey For The Bees' with its asymmetrical rising synth sequence). Duran Duran used an arpeggiator in their hit single 'Rio' (1982).

Roland MC-4: This was a pre-MIDI sequencer that used control voltage signals to control synthesisers and/or drum machines. The MC-500 was perhaps Roland's most popular MIDI sequencer.

Roland MC-4

MUSICAL EXAMPLE

DURAN DURAN, 'RIO' (1982)

This song features an arpeggiator, a function on a synthesiser (in this case a Roland Jupiter-4) which uses in-built clocks, or timing signals, from an external device such as a drum-machine, to divide up the notes of a chord held down by the player and play them one at a time sweeping up, down or randomly and in regular durations. In this song the semiquaver loops created are prominent during the introduction and verse, and particularly effective when used as a solo break before the vocal chorus.

The song begins with a sustained electronic sound produced by reversed loops of metal rods bouncing on the strings of a grand piano.

0:18 Four bars of arpeggiator notes are accompanied by the drum kit playing tom toms, and a fast-moving bass line.

0:25 An electric guitar joins in, playing heavy chords on beats 2 and 4, and the intro continues with drums settling into a regular semiquaver beat on high hats and offbeat snare.

0:39 The vocals enter with a regularly phrased 16-bar verse.

1:10 The main vocals are joined by backing vocals for the chorus, which follows the harmonic sequence: E I B I D I A I in a regular four-by-four structure.

1:37 An instrumental link based on the intro takes us to

1:50 verse 2, which leads to chorus 2 and then

2:48 a more mellow section, when for the first time the arpeggiator drops out and the drums maintain the semiquaver feel quietly on hats.

3:01 A tenor sax takes on a substantial solo.

3:43 An adapted verse is followed by two choruses and the sax returns – this time the vocalists join in, and a coda section finishes the song with slowed-down emphatic chords at the end.

Duran Duran

At this time many pop dance bands, such as Frankie Goes To Hollywood ('Relax', 1984), were produced by Trevor Horn – a particularly successful musician and record producer, who had began his career in a group called The Buggles.

Duran Duran adopted a highly fashionable image and their style became known as the new romantics. Other new romantic bands included Spandau Ballet and Culture Club. Even with these groups, guitars remained subordinate to synthesisers.

RISE OF THE POP VIDEO

The promotional video that supported Duran Duran's 'Rio' was shot on a yacht speeding around the Caribbean. The pop video had now become an essential part of marketing for many groups. The first video to be entirely shot and edited on video-tape was Queen's 'Bohemian Rhapsody' (1975). When MTV launched in the USA in 1981 (and the UK in 1987) the TV channel was constantly looking for new material, and the opportunity for additional airtime could not be missed. Adam and the Ants, a punk-orientated new romantic group, had particular success on MTV ('Prince Charming', 1981). The BBC's TV programme *Old Grey Whistle Test* produced some of its own videos, but on *Top of the Pops* there was a strict limit to the number allowed each week. The video for Michael Jackson's 'Thriller', produced in 1983, was a short film directed by John Landis, and featured ghoulish special effects with Michael and his zombie undead followers dancing to terrify his girlfriend. The title single to the follow-up album *Bad* (1987) had a video directed by the famous film director Martin Scorsese.

A-ha, a Norwegian synthpop group, won several awards for the groundbreaking video to promote their song 'Take On Me' (1985), which explored the interface between pencil drawings and the real world. Peter Gabriel's innovative video for 'Sledgehammer' (1986) used plasticine animation made at the studios of Aardman Animation, soon to become home to Wallace and Gromit.

The Pet Shop Boys' videos were a good example of the high-quality productions of the time. Their hit 'It's A Sin' (1987), directed by Derek Jarman, features their vocalist Neil Tennant in chains while judgemental monks parade the seven deadly sins before him. 'Heart', from the same album (*Actually*, 1987) used a vampire theme in its video, based on the 1922 film *Nosferatu*. Directed by Jack Bond, it was shot in Slovenia.

MUSICAL EXAMPLE

PET SHOP BOYS, 'HEART'
(1988)

The Pet Shop Boys

In addition to the live recordings there are a number of different mixes of this song: a studio mix, an extended dance mix, an album mix and video mix as well as the original single release. This section concentrates on the last of these, which begins with:

■ a four-on-the-floor bass drum thud, with repeated sequenced semiquaver notes on the drum synth (A).

0:03   Synth quavers are added that follow the harmony an octave higher (B) and high electronic tom toms continue (C).

0:19   Synth-strings layered with choir pad now come into the mix, playing sustained chords (D).

0:27   A synth vocal lead sound plays a riff in the middle of this increasingly complex texture, which based around A minor with the Aeolian G♮ (see p. 29) at the end of the bar (E).

0:33   Then little bursts of sampled strings punctuate the ends of phrases (F).

This adds up to a total intro of 22 bars, as set out below:

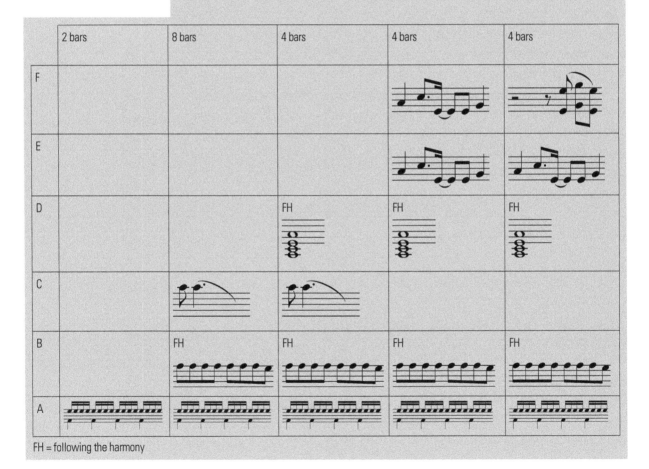

FH = following the harmony

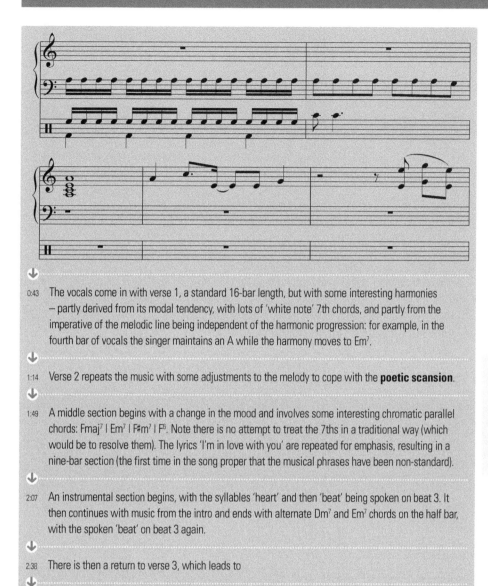

0:43   The vocals come in with verse 1, a standard 16-bar length, but with some interesting harmonies – partly derived from its modal tendency, with lots of 'white note' 7th chords, and partly from the imperative of the melodic line being independent of the harmonic progression: for example, in the fourth bar of vocals the singer maintains an A while the harmony moves to Em⁷.

1:14   Verse 2 repeats the music with some adjustments to the melody to cope with the **poetic scansion**.

1:49   A middle section begins with a change in the mood and involves some interesting chromatic parallel chords: Fmaj⁷ | Em⁷ | F♯m⁷ | F⁶. Note there is no attempt to treat the 7ths in a traditional way (which would be to resolve them). The lyrics 'I'm in love with you' are repeated for emphasis, resulting in a nine-bar section (the first time in the song proper that the musical phrases have been non-standard).

2:07   An instrumental section begins, with the syllables 'heart' and then 'beat' being spoken on beat 3. It then continues with music from the intro and ends with alternate Dm⁷ and Em⁷ chords on the half bar, with the spoken 'beat' on beat 3 again.

2:38   There is then a return to verse 3, which leads to

3:09   a repeat of the middle section and then on to

3:30   the coda, made up from spoken syllables 'heart beat' and a return of the high synth toms.

✳️
Poetic scansion: The patterns of stressed and unstressed syllables in poetry or lyrics, such as:

yŏu Múst ŭndĕrstánd
thrŏugh thĕ Tóuch
ŏf yŏur hánd

As the decade progressed, music technology made rapid advances. When The Human League released their synthpop hit single 'Don't You Want Me' in 1982, and its accompanying album *Dare*, their synth program was played by a step-time sequencer. More sophisticated MIDI hardware and software then became available which, rather than increasing the de-humanised element, released bands from the slavishness of step-time loops and allowed them to integrate more real instruments into their compositions. If singles such as Depeche Mode's 'Just Can't Get Enough' (1981) are compared with later tracks – for example, 'Love In Itself' from their *Construction Time Again* album, only two years later in 1983 – the more complex textures and darker sound of the later work can easily be identified.

Emulator II

MUSICAL INSTRUMENT

THE SAMPLER

One piece of revolutionary music technology hardware that became available in the 1980s was the sampler. The Fairlight CMI and the Synclavier were expensive computer systems that had used sampling technology since the end of the 1970s but now the E-mu Emulator was available, particularly the mark II released in 1984.

A sampler can 'record' or capture and store an acoustic sound using digital technology. This allows the sound to be 'triggered', either through MIDI connections or by an integrated music keyboard which can play the recording (or sample) back, stop playing it on key release or keep playing it in a continuous loop when the key is held down. As the sample is triggered from higher or lower notes on the keyboard, the result begins to sound unnatural. Therefore if the player requires the sound to retain its original character, several samples of the original source need to be taken, and stored in different 'zones' across the keyboard.

A sample can be processed using synthesiser parameters, joined to another sample, or cut into sections to be triggered by different notes from the keyboard (called keyboard mapping). It became possible to time-stretch samples (make them shorter or longer) without affecting their pitch. Triggering a single sound is known as a one-shot, and some drum samplers are optimised for this. Samples can be stored — initially on removable floppy discs, later on built-in hard drives — or transferred to a computer for editing or storage.

Paul Hardcastle demonstrated the novel elements of samplers when he hired an Emulator and produced a single called '19'. Its immediate attraction was the stuttering effect ('n-n-n-nineteen') caused by repeatedly triggering the spoken word 'nineteen' sample, although other samples such as the voices of US soldiers and a military bugle call were used to fit with the single's serious subject — war in Vietnam. A radio documentary reporter giving a running commentary was used to give both structural cohesion and narrative authenticity.

In 1986 Akai began producing the first truly affordable samplers, and in 1987 the release of the E-mu SP-1200 percussion sampler offered an alternative to the drum machine for producers.

HIP HOP

US hip-hop composers wholeheartedly adopted sampling technology, as it was much easier to use than twin turntables. Hip-hop culture developed in the northern part of New York known as the Bronx at the end of the 1970s. It featured urban graffiti, dancing, and party music played by DJs on mobile soundsystems, taking ideas from Jamaica and using MCs to host events, who would often talk over the music. Two side-by-side record turntables were connected to substantial amplification systems, in the early days sometimes plugged into a streetlight power supply. Partygoers particularly enjoyed the instrumental breaks in the funk, Latin and rock records being played, and the DJs would use the same record on both their turntables so that they quickly repeated the crowd's favourite section, being so skilful at this that the join became unnoticeable. Soon a style of music resulted where by the DJs' repeated breaks were the dominant factor, along with MCs improvising spoken lyrics or poetry that became known as 'rap'. Young people created novel dance moves to the style, and became known as breakdancers.

Pioneers of the hip-hop style DJ Kool Herc and Afrika Bambaataa are often credited with bringing a more positive attitude to life in the Bronx. Grand Wizzard Theodore and DJ Grandmaster Flash introduced the idea of moving the turntable backwards and forwards with the needle on the record, creating a percussive sound known as scratching. In addition, a mixer was used to 'cue up' the right section of the record without the audience hearing, and so the DJ would normally be seen wearing headphones. Soon record producers realised there might be a commercial potential in hip hop and the first 'records of records' were made. Sugar Hill Records, founded in 1978, were specialists in rap music, producing 'Rapper's Delight' for the Sugarhill Gang in 1979, the first commercial hip-hop hit.

MUSICAL EXAMPLE

GRANDMASTER FLASH AND THE FURIOUS FIVE, 'THE MESSAGE' (1982)

The tempo of this highly successful single and album track was slower than normal (103bpm), helping to focus on the message of the lyrics, which concentrated on life in the ghetto. In their album *The Adventures of Grandmaster Flash on the Wheels of Steel* (1981), samples were taken from Blondie and Queen tracks, among others. In 'The Message', the band sample themselves using the vocals from their 1979 track "Superrappin".

Grandmaster Flash

The track begins with a repeated two-bar bass synth riff and heavy drumbeat produced on an Oberheim DMX drum machine, and a reversed cymbal crash that has the effect of building up instead of dying down.

0:04 Echo delays on rising and falling synth lines mixed with percussion samples and assorted synth notes enter, leading to the vocal rap:

0:43 'It's like a jungle sometimes, it makes me wonder how I keep from going under', which serves as a refrain for the song.

0:52 After these, the backing track continues for four bars with other interesting sounds, including a triplet on closed high hats.

1:01 The rap verse begins, listing in semiquaver patter the problems of living in the black ghetto. This leads to strongly emphasised lyrics in a crotchet triplet rhythm:

1:20 'Don't push me cos I'm close to the edge.' This line is frequently followed by mock laughter delivered rhythmically.

There are five verses of lyrics, with each verse getting longer, and with choruses between them.

6:17 The track finishes with street-corner conversation, traffic noise and sounds of a police arrest overdubbing the backing track.

Other hip-hop artists such as Ice Cube and Puff Daddy sampled the synthesiser riff on 'The Message'. The track is so successful because of a combination of factors: the heavy dance beat, the lyrics and their rhythmic delivery, and the funky backing track with its novel use of synths and samples.

In 1986 Run-DMC produced the album *Raising Hell*, which proved the commercial viability of hip hop with its crossover success. The single 'Walk This Way' was a cover of the 1970s rock band Aerosmith's original single, produced jointly with Aerosmith in the studio and featured on a 'making of' video. Run-DMC's version helped to revitalise the rock band's career and is also credited as helping rap breakthrough into the mainstream.

HEAVY METAL

Following on from the tradition set by Led Zeppelin and Deep Purple was a difficult job for bands involved in the heavy rock idiom. The punk revolution had stolen the limelight, and even the post-punk bands had a different approach to music-making. Theirs was more commercially conscious than the more do-it-yourself approach of the high-energy and heavily amplified sound that became known as heavy metal music. The band Motörhead is recognised as bridging the gap between punk and heavy metal when they were formed in 1975, but the genre was not to break into the mainstream until the 1980s.

Below is a list of some of the influential heavy metal bands from the late 1970s and 80s, together with an example of one of their most successful albums and the subgenre they most clearly fit in.

Band	Album	Year	Subgenre
Kiss	*Love Gun*	1977	US stadium
Aerosmith	*Pump*	1989	
Motörhead	*Ace of Spades*	1980	New wave of British heavy metal
Judas Priest	*British Steel*	1980	
Iron Maiden	*The Number of the Beast*	1982	
Def Leppard	*Hysteria*	1987	
Twisted Sister	*Stay Hungry*	1984	Hair metal
Metallica	*...and Justice for All*	1988	Thrash metal
Megadeth	*Countdown to Extinction*	1992	

Other identified subgenres of heavy metal that grew up in the 1980s include death metal, black metal, power metal and gothic metal. The Cure was a band that began in a post-punk style, but during the 1980s their music became progressively darker and they adopted both a gothic image and a more accessible sound than some, making them the most commercially successful in the genre.

Heavy metal grew from the twin roots of psychedelic and blues rock, with an element of rebellious youth that rivalled punk, although its fans were more generally to be found among the urban working class. With the exception of a few bands that continued to produce music at the same speed as some of Black Sabbath's Doom Metal songs, tempi were very fast and avoided jerky syncopations, being driven by powerful bass lines and large drum kits. Electric guitars played **power chords** and low-pitched riffs that often held the song structures together, or let fly with high screaming solos demonstrating their prowess. Compared with earlier hard rock styles the language was less blues-based and more frequently used minor modes. Tunes still used modal phrases, particularly the Aeolian and **Phrygian**. Lyrics were often based on fantasy or mythological themes, and the uniform of black printed t-shirts and long hair was essential.

Power chords: Chords played on an electric guitar that leave out the third and usually move in repeated or parallel motion.

Phrygian: The mode beginning on E.

MUSICAL EXAMPLE

MOTÖRHEAD, 'ACE OF SPADES' (1980)

The English band Motörhead released this single as the title track of their 1980 album and a preview for an autumn UK tour. Even though they had only three members, the band made a powerful sound.

Motörhead

The song begins with an up-tempo distorted bass playing repeated quavers and sounding more like a lead guitar. The drums enter with a heavy semiquaver beat using just the snare.

0:05   The lead guitar riff begins, also heavily distorted and based on repeated Es, including the instrument's sixth (bottom open) string, while sliding down two frets on the fourth string:

0:12   The harmony moves up a minor third and the vocals enter based on a high repeated G.

0:20   The four bars of the opening E riff return.

0:26   Vocals continue with the second line of lyrics, this time based over D and C chords but the vocal line only moves to F♯ for the D chord, then rises back up to G.

0:29   The four bars of the E riff return.

0:33   Vocals continue with a repeat of the music from the second line, but this time extended to chant out the song titles.

0:43   A second verse begins with the same music and new lyrics.

1:18   More lines of lyrics are then treated in stop time: a moment for the drummer to gather his breath after maintaining a constant driving beat, and a chance for the vocalist to get his devil-may-care gambling message across.

1:27   The harmony slides down to D and then B to take us back to the key chord E for

1:31   an extended guitar solo,

1:58   verse 3 and

2:26   a coda that concludes the song, beginning with Em harmony then moving down to D and C and finishing the song with E, D, E parallel power chords.

Heavy metal bands from the 1980s included Iron Maiden, Saxon, Diamond Head (all part of the new wave of British heavy metal) and their musical offspring in the thrash/speed metal of Metallica, Megadeth, and Slayer. The 'hair' metal of the Los Angeles bands – such as Poison, Guns N' Roses or Mötley Crüe – was slickly produced music, combining elements of the heavier bands with an updated version of 1970s hard rock to create a very commercially successful sound. The LA bands had a penchant for make-up and power ballads (Poison's 'Every Rose Has Its Thorn' is a prime example), which were anathema to bands such as Metallica.

MUSICAL EXAMPLE

GUNS N' ROSES, 'SWEET CHILD O' MINE' (1987)

Compared with the Motörhead example on page 85, this track uses a cleaner, less distorted guitar style and a less driving pulse. The band can be classed as a hard rock group although the distinctions between the various subgenres of rock music at this time were blurred.

The music begins with a high electric guitar riff based on repeated quavers, of which only the first changes, in every other bar:

0:15 The guitar riff repeats as the drums enter with a roll and a crash, and the bass guitar plays a high melodic phrase.

0:30 The drums break into a rock rhythm while the guitar riff continues to repeat, and the bass and rhythm guitar provide a harmony of D I D I C I C I G I G I D I D :ll

0:45 Axel Rose's powerful tenor vocals enter with a gradually descending melody for the first eight bars of the song, repeated for a further eight.

1:16 The song title appears as the lyrics of a short chorus for two repeated four-bar phrases over a change in harmony to A I C I D I D :ll, with the lead guitar riff featuring over the D chords.

1:30 There is then an expressive eight-bar lead guitar solo, leading to

1:46 verse 2 and the second chorus, then

2:32 a longer guitar solo extended to 16 bars, and

3:03 repeats of the chorus.

3:35 A key change to Em begins an extended guitar solo.

4:38 New music, based on the lyrics 'Where do we go?' uttered darkly in a lower pitch, provides a contrast and, as the guitar solo continues frenetically above, this section turns out to be a finishing coda.

UK ROCK BRANCHES OUT

Some bands from the UK rock scene need to be mentioned at this point. The Smiths, whose *Meat is Murder* from 1985 reached number 1 in the album charts, and later the Stone Roses and the Happy Mondays all hailed from Manchester. With their mixture of dance and rock these bands were important influences on alternative rock and indie bands in the following decade. In addition, partly because of the immigrant population in the UK, Jamaican music continued to influence rock performers. Reggae-influenced bands included UB40 ('Red, Red Wine', 1983) and The Police, whose vocalist and bass player Sting was fond of reggae-style melodic bass lines (for example 'Can't Stand Losin' You', 1979), drummer Stewart Copeland used third-beat emphasis with lots of **rim shots** (for example 'Don't Stand So Close To Me', 1980) and guitarist Andy Summers enjoyed skank guitar offbeats (for example 'Walking On The Moon', 1979). In 1983 The Police produced the single 'Every Breath You Take', which topped the UK charts for four weeks and the US *Billboard* hot 100 charts for eight, subsequently winning several awards.

Rim shots: Drumming technique that uses a stick played hard against both the metal rim and the head of the drum simultaneously, creating a sound like a rifle shot.

MUSICAL EXAMPLE	
THE POLICE, 'EVERY BREATH YOU TAKE' (1983)	A gentle picked guitar pattern that changes with the harmonies begins the music, together with a rock rhythm on drums with a strong offbeat, and a bass guitar playing quavers on the root notes of the chords.

00:14 Section A: Sting's vocals enter utilising a small range of four melody notes from G up to C over a repeat of the harmonies from the introduction, with an interrupted cadence at the end of the first line: chord V (D) moves to chord VI (Em) instead of chord I (G) as it would in a 'perfect' cadence.

00:31 Line 2 of the verse.

00:48 Section B: a new vocal line rises higher and begins with chord IV harmonies, moving back down to G via a B♭ blues note in the bass. To finish, this section moves through a chord of A⁷ – a secondary dominant (see p. 21) – and ends on D.

1:04 The opening melody returns (section A).

1:22 Section C: a change of key to E♭ major launches into a new section, with a more electric sound created by guitar chords at the start of every two bars, although the quaver movement is maintained by the bass.

1:43 A section without vocals begins although there is no big instrumental solo but simple processed guitar chords on the offbeats.

2:14 A return to section B.

2:30 A return to section A.

2:46 A tag repeat of the last three bars of section A begins a coda section that features backing vocals repeating the lyrics of the opening line, and the song concludes with a gradual fade-out.

The song structure is therefore: AABACABA, a structure unusual for pop music and similar to some classical music rondo forms.

Other bands were influenced by the early form of reggae called ska (see p. 48), and the record label 2 Tone gave its name to a British ska revival, recording bands such as The Specials ('Ghost Town', 1981) and Madness ('House Of Fun', 1982). Madness was particularly successful from the late 1970s through to 1988 as they adopted a pop style, but they never lost their Jamaican influence, heard in their reggae rhythms and horn section.

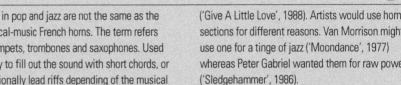

MUSICAL INSTRUMENT

HORN SECTION

Horns in pop and jazz are not the same as the classical-music French horns. The term refers to trumpets, trombones and saxophones. Used mostly to fill out the sound with short chords, or occasionally lead riffs depending of the musical genre, they can be found in a whole variety of genres. However, they are a particular feature of R&B-influenced styles such as funk, soul and gospel, together with Jamaican ska and rocksteady, and Latin dance and pop genres (for example, Gloria Estefan and Miami Sound Machine, 'Conga', 1985).

Touring bands would sometimes carry their own horn section rather than employ session musicians, such as the British reggae bands UB40 (featuring Chrissie Hynde, 'I Got You Babe', 1985) and Aswad

('Give A Little Love', 1988). Artists would use horn sections for different reasons. Van Morrison might use one for a tinge of jazz ('Moondance', 1977) whereas Peter Gabriel wanted them for raw power ('Sledgehammer', 1986).

Trumpets provide the top screech, and when used through a microphone cut through the sound of the electric instruments well. Jazz big-band players are used to very high notes, and pop bands would often employ jazz session musicians. Trombones could double trumpets to provide depth. Saxes blend well and are ideal for smooth accompanying chords, but equally can provide growling power solos through a microphone. However, most often the players would work as a team.

Remember that trumpets and saxes are transposing instruments. Trumpets sound a tone lower than written, alto saxes a major 6th lower than written, and tenors an octave and a tone lower. Short notes are played even shorter than written unless they are marked with a ⁻ symbol.

Horn section

MUSICAL EXAMPLE

MADNESS, 'UNCLE SAM' (1985)

This is a track from the critically acclaimed album *Mad not Mad* (1985) and was released as a single along with 'Yesterday's Men'. It is highly inventive, particularly in terms of rhythms and sound effects, and the horn section makes a valuable contribution.

Madness

The track begins with the sound of a ship's fog horn, tuned to a low F – the song's key is E major.

0:05   A snare drum fill leads straight into the main song. Heavy stress is laid on beats 2 and 4 by snare drum and keyboards while the bass plays a quaver figure that stops short of beat 3. This bass pattern is consistent throughout most of the song and gives it a light bouncy feel, part of the reggae influence.

The melody is constructed from four repeated four-bar phrases with the rhythm changing to accommodate the novel lyrics (such as 'knockety knock, knocking upon my door' – mirrored in the percussion with knocking on woodblocks).

0:35   The verse continues with a change in harmony to chord V (B major) and the melody still based on short phrases. The horn section echoes the melody line with staccato semiquavers. After eight bars the vocals repeatedly stress a D♮, giving a bluesy lead into

1:04   the chorus based on the key chord E, in which the horn section provides chordal accompaniment. The chorus concludes with a rhythmic tutti on the words 'to be with my Uncle Sam' and a drum fill made from rim shots.

1:23   Verse 2 begins, which includes more rhythmic interjections from the horns and ends with an organ glissando leading into

1:58   the second chorus.

2:12   This finishes by suddenly twisting to C major (♮VI) a busy eight bars of sound effects and a **Wagner**-inspired fanfare.

2:27   The chorus returns and leads to the second half of the verse and a final chorus fade-out, with a double-time percussion feel and a heavy reverberated snare drum sounding like **timbales**.

The song is a production tour-de-force, although it is reported that the band were unhappy with the slick studio techniques used.

Wagner, Richard: German composer 1813–83 who composed mostly Romantic-style operas based on Scandinavian sagas and German folk tales, famed for his integration of drama and music and his skilful use of the orchestra.

Timbales: Shallow single-headed drums about the size of a snare drum and made of metal. Originated in Cuba.

1980s SUPERSTARS

The rise of cable TV in the USA, and in particular MTV, was important in the career of several pop artists who were to become global superstars during the 1980s. Three particular artists were able to capitalise on the power of this new promotional medium using both their skills in dance and imaginative production ideas to put across their music.

    Michael Jackson's dancing skills were evident from his younger days as the front-line vocalist with the Jackson 5. He even had a solo hit of his own aged just 14 ('Rockin'

Robin', 1972). His song 'Billie Jean' (1982), with its looping bass line and offbeat claps, is credited as breaking the colour barrier on MTV as it was the first by a non-white to get regular plays (MTV was dependent on record companies for their videos and it was thought that videos of black music would not help sales). In the video for this song he perfected his Moonwalk – a medium-tempo athletic dance involving slides and gyrations. 'Billie Jean' was a single from the album *Thriller*, and Jackson's skilful music arranger Quincy Jones helped him to produce the 14-minute video based on the album's title track a year later. It wasn't an easy job to follow the *Thriller* album, but in 1987 the *Bad* album proved Michael Jackson's longevity.

Five of the singles released from *Bad* became number-one hits, and a brief summary of their characteristics is set out below:

Thriller became the world's best-selling album of all time. Seven of its nine tracks were released as singles – all reaching the US top 10.

Orchestra hit: Sample of a whole orchestra playing a single chord that is triggered by a keyboard or sequencer, and so can move up or down creating parallel harmonies.

Track number	Song title	Music and production
1	'Bad'	After four rising **orchestra hits** a bass synthesiser riff starts that runs through most of the song using a compelling syncopation created by moving the first note of the repeated second bar away from the downbeat. Sequenced semiquavers repeat a non-pitch tone that pans between left and right channels a bar at a time. Like many of the tracks of the album it uses a gated offbeat snare (see p. 57).
2	'The Way You Make Me Feel'	Beginning with a motorbike sample and synth tom toms, the music sets off in a medium-tempo rock shuffle with a heavy triplet, two-beat synth bass. Parallel chords of F and E♭ provide a harmonic support for Jackson's bluesy vocals. Electronically processed backing vocals are used in a call-and-response chorus.
7	'Man In The Mirror'	Reverberant electric piano patterns solo at the start with finger clicks, and vocals enter this light texture, the second line in harmony. A kick drum provides a medium-tempo beat leading to a catchy chorus. A heavier offbeat gated electric snare is added for verse 2, and after a second chorus there is a key change up from G to A♭, and a gospel choir provides a fuller texture while Jackson continues his soulful vocal improvisations. A long coda concludes the song.
8	'I Just Can't Stop Loving You'	High, atmospheric strings lead into a heartfelt ballad with Jackson's vocals accompanied by electric piano. A steady medium-light rock tempo is established, leading to a chorus. A middle section is reached introducing the voice of Siedah Garrett, later used for duet answering phrasing with Jackson.
9	'Dirty Diana'	The track begins with layered, metallic-sounding samples creating a menacing atmosphere. A dark bass-line ostinato is created using G I E♭ F: II The track is in a hard-rock style using electric guitar licks and a powerful solo near the end, although strings also fill out the texture.

Michael Jackson

Quincy Jones employs a range of production tricks to make the music interesting, and Jackson's compelling performances enhanced by the dramatic videos ensured its success.

Madonna was trained as a professional dancer and this is clearly evident in the highly complex stage shows she toured with to promote her music. Her videos were highly imaginative, often exploring issues of sexuality, religion/spirituality and consumer society. Some of the compositional techniques used by Madonna are:

- A four-on-the-floor acoustic or electronic kick-drum bass beat ('Holiday',1983)
- Up-tempo dance numbers using constant semiquaver drum and synth notes ('Express Yourself', 1989; 'Vogue', 1990)
- Synthesiser loops ('Material Girl', 1985; 'Like A Virgin', 1984; 'Into The Groove', 1985)
- Songs of empowerment ('Express Yourself', 1989)
- A slow introduction outlining the subject matter ('Like A Prayer', 1989)
- Imaginative orchestrations (string orchestra music in 'Papa Don't Preach', 1986, or Latin percussion and Spanish guitars in 'La Isla Bonita', 1987).

Madonna

Trying to categorise Madonna is difficult as she continually re-invented herself, staying at the cutting edge of music fashions. She was at home with power ballads ('Live to Tell', 1986), and even took the lead part in the 1996 film of Andrew Lloyd Webber's musical *Evita*. Many of Madonna's hits were produced by Shep Pettibone, who also worked with George Michael, the Pet Shop Boys and Janet Jackson.

Prince was very much a one-man band. Not only was he a highly skilled performer, often playing all the instruments on a track, but also he wrote his own songs and produced his own records and videos. His style derives from 1970s funk artists such as George Clinton and Parliament (see p. 65), which he blended with a pop language of his own. His major breakthrough into the pop charts came with the release of his album *1999* (1982), from which the singles '1999' and 'Little Red Corvette' were taken. The latter was played in rotation on MTV along with Michael Jackson's 'Billie Jean'.

Prince

In 1984 Prince produced the film *Purple Rain*, and the soundtrack album from this is highly regarded. The album mixes a variety of styles, including pop, rock, R&B and dance, using a richer texture largely because Prince used a backing band to fill out the sound. Singles from the album include 'Let's Go Crazy' – a fast dance number that charges to a sudden break with an unaccompanied guitar solo followed by a vaudeville-style ending – and the title track, a soulful power ballad. Prince continued to make successful albums through the 1980s with *Around The World In A Day* (1985), *Parade* (1986 – another soundtrack album) and *Sign o' the Times* (1987), for which he abandoned his group The Revolution and went solo, taking on a style that owed less to rock and more to soul. He had particular success in the UK and Europe at the turn of the decade, the *Lovesexy* album (1988) being promoted with a world tour. Prince produced successful albums through the 1990s and up to the present.

Mark Knopfler from Dire Straits

Dire Straits

One British band that was successful on MTV was Dire Straits. They had had a huge hit with their first released single ('Sultans Of Swing', 1978; re-released 1979) on both sides of the Atlantic, but ironically it was the song 'Money For Nothing' (1984) – which criticises consumer society, including MTV – that was the first music video to be played on MTV Europe. The video also made use of early computer graphics to illustrate its message. It was taken from the album *Brothers in Arms*, which was a landmark in recording history being produced using only digital technology (DDD). The title track is reputed to be the world's first CD single, and the album the first to outsell its LP (vinyl) version. The music from the album is a mixture of the clean bluesy rock of their earlier work together with the more folk-influenced language used, for example, by the title track. It was written by the band's lead guitarist and front-line vocalist Mark Knopfler.

Major pentatonic scale: Starting on C this five-note scale would be C, D, E, G, A. It is common in indigenous folk music throughout the world.

Suspensions: Notes held over while chords change, usually creating tension that is released in the following chords.

MUSICAL EXAMPLE

DIRE STRAITS, 'BROTHERS IN ARMS' (1985)

This song is a dreamlike ballad based on an anti-war theme. The sound of the lead guitar is present throughout. Knopfler played a Gibson Les Paul guitar on the recording, without the usual guitarist's heavy distortion but processed with some reverb and sustain.

The music begins with a short introduction using sustained organ chords, with Mark Knopfler's expressive lead guitar playing providing short solo phrases above. There is also the dark sound of thunder or possible distant gunfire rumbling in the background.

0:31 The introduction concludes and the vocals enter with 'These mist covered mountains are home to me now', using Mark Knopfler's close-miked baritone voice.

The melody of the verse is largely **major pentatonic**. (In the song's key of B, the note E is used only twice, once as a passing note and once at the end to emphasise the word 'Brothers', and A♯ is avoided altogether. This avoids the harsh-sounding tritone.)

Sustained organ chords continue, using **suspensions** (reminiscent of church music) to help to maintain a reverent atmosphere, while the guitar provides musical comment between lines of the lyrics. Knopler uses a range of playing techniques, including string bends, hammer-ons (see p. 25) and fading in the sound with the volume control, thus avoiding the hard-picked attack.

1:16 Verses 1 and 2 are linked with a short instrumental passage similar to the intro.

1:33 Verse 2 adds a gentle drum-kit beat and ends with another instrumental interlude, leading to

2:34 a middle section where the melody phrases are shorter and the guitar licks more frequent, concluding with a longer guitar solo.

3:29 Verse 3 is delivered, and the song ends with a more substantial guitar solo and fade-out.

UK FEMALE VOCALISTS

Alongside Madonna, Whitney Houston, Tina Turner and Cyndi Lauper from the USA, and Gloria Estefan from Cuba, a number of British female singers had particular success during the 1980s. Annie Lennox was the lead vocalist of the Eurythmics ('Sweet Dreams Are Made Of This', 1983), a new wave duo that used synth pop backing, with David A. Stewart playing guitar and producing the synth backing tracks used so much on the band's records. Annie Lennox had a rich and dark **alto** voice and a forceful personality that stood her in good stead when she embarked on a successful solo career in the 1990s.

Alto: Low female voice.

Kate Bush had a number-one hit with her first single 'Wuthering Heights' in 1978. As the 1980s progressed she proved herself to be an original singer-songwriter with a unique vocal style and storytelling lyrics. Her music used unusual acoustic instruments which, when combined with modern electronics, produced a wholly original soundscape. For example, in the album *The Sensual World* (1989) there were strings and folk fiddles, mandolins and **bouzoukis**, and Irish pipes and whistles, alongside drums, bass and a Fairlight sampler. Well-known musicians wanted to take part in her projects, and on this album can be found her friend and mentor Dave Gilmour from Pink Floyd playing guitar, with the film composer Michael Kamen writing some of the orchestrations. She influenced many female artists of later generations including Tori Amos, Alison Goldfrapp, the Icelandic singer Björk and later Florence and the Machine.

Bouzouki: Stringed instrument from Greece, with a pear-shaped body. Related to the lute.

CELTIC FUSION

Kate Bush was not the only artist in the 1980s to produce pop or rock music that had a folk-roots influence. In 1982 the Irish band Clannad had a huge international hit with a close-harmony ballad entitled 'Theme From Harry's Game', written for a Yorkshire TV drama series based on the troubles in Northern Ireland. Clannad's expressive music showed how modern recording techniques could smooth over the raw edges of traditional folk music and bring it to a wider audience. The band went on to provide more music for television drama in the form of *Robin of Sherwood*, and for this they used even more polished production techniques, including a greater use of synthesisers. Their lead singer Enya went on to have a successful solo career, with several hit albums, and also provided some music for the soundtrack of the *Lord of the Rings* film trilogy. There had been successful attempts to produce electric folk music in the 1970s with bands such as Steeleye Span and Fairport Convention, but Clannad and later Enya's glossy production values took Celtic fusion to new levels of artistry. Other Celtic fusion artists from the 1980s and early 1990s include Sinéad O'Connor, the Pogues (whose style can be described as Celtic punk), The Corrs and the Scottish band Capercaillie. The characteristics of the style include a wide use of pentatonic scales and an often less aggressive mood than rock music.

The music for *Harry's Game* is a good example of juxtapostion, where Clannad's beautiful music is a stark contrast to shootings on the streets of Belfast.

Kate Bush

STOCK, AITKEN AND WATERMAN

Like Holland-Dozier-Holland from the 1960s Motown hit factory, the British songwriting team of Stock, Aitken and Waterman (SAW) were known for their high-quality commercial sound, which produced hits for a number of artists through the decade. They would choose a song title, lay down a guide rhythm using a Linn 9000 drum-machine track, create a harmonic structure with a keyboard track, add the bass, guitars, synths and percussion and then finally bring in a singer to record the vocals. According to Les Sharma, an engineer at Peter Waterman's south London PWL studios, the team used a Sony 24-track digital tape recorder that used ½-inch tape. Vocals were usually recorded with a Calrec stereo microphone and EQed, de-essed and processed with dynamic compression (see p. 128) on their way in to the **SSL** desk. This processing resulted in a glossy sound, where the natural rough edges of the vocal line were smoothed over.

SSL: Abbreviation for Solid State Logic, a manufacturer of commercial recording-studio equipment.

The high-tempo music the team produced became known as Hi-NRG (high energy), and was influenced by European disco styles.

SAW's somewhat formulaic approach made celebrity pop singers of the Australian soap stars Kylie Minogue and Jason Donovan, along with many other artists including Rick Astley and Bananarama. Although music critics disliked their approach, the result was more than 100 UK top-forty hits, and global sales of about 40 million units.

DEVELOPMENTS IN MUSIC TECHNOLOGY

- The advances in synthesiser technology during the decade paralleled the musical styles of synthpop and new wave:
    - Polyphonic synthesisers became cheaper and easier to program, with presets, memory locations and onboard effects.
    - Yamaha produced their range of Digital FM synths, including the moderately priced DX7 in 1983, noted for its electronic piano and marimba sounds. FM synthesis uses carrier and modulator combinations as in FM radio, and sound character is more accurately represented numerically rather than with haphazard analogue controls.
    - Roland produced the D-50 in 1987, which uses linear arithmetic synthesis. This is a system whereby the very beginning of a sound is sampled (the attack transient) and normal analogue oscillators produce the rest. The idea is that the human ear picks up the quality of a sound from its very beginning and so is fooled into thinking it's a real instrument.
- In 1980 Simmons electronic drums were produced.
- 1981 saw the production of the Roland TR-808 analogue drum machine, which was the mainstay of many dance and hip-hop tracks of the decade.
- The E-Mu Emulator II keyboard workstation was produced, a relatively affordable sampler, able to produce eight sounds simultaneously (eight-part multi-timbral).

- Aftertouch featured on many moderately priced syths (the ability to change a sound by applying pressure to a key after it has been depressed).
- Steinberg produced their Pro-24 sequencer software for the Atari-ST computer, which was to develop later into the Cubase family. Atari computers were favourites with musicians; they had a fast processor for the time and built-in MIDI ports.
- 1982 the first 5-inch CD audio discs were marketed.
- 1985 CD-ROMs were invented.
- 1987 Digital Audio Tape (DAT) was introduced.
- 1988 CD sales surpass vinyl LPs.

CHAPTER 6

The 1990s

BACKGROUND

There was an increasing diversification of music genres throughout the 1990s, and an individualist and entrepreneurial approach to the arts encouraged by governments in both the USA and the UK contributed to this. Sometimes, however, a counter-cultural reaction against the commercial methods of the music industry set in, disagreeing with glossy production and MTV-orientated pop (the Seattle 'grunge' style is one example of such a reaction; see p. 98). At other times the technology-driven innovations that sprung up during the decade were wholeheartedly embraced by artists, who used them to produce music that was both futuristic and exciting (for example in the electronic and dance genres).

The information revolution and the development of technologies that eventually were to have a profound effect on the music industry were now under way. The internet became more widely available, and developments in computer systems allowed software houses to write programs that not just professional recording engineers but also the home enthusiast could use. In 1998 both the Apple iMac computer and the Windows 98 platforms were released, and their user-friendly environments made music software even easier to use for both recording and composing music.

The music CD format was now firmly established, with DVD hot on its heels (introduced in the USA in 1997), and record companies realised that there was a market for re-releasing their original LP recordings in digital format, with CDs being both more portable and durable than vinyl. Singles could be re-released as compilation albums, and artists that were still around were easily persuaded to add a few extra new tracks, a live recording or at least a new studio mix to the contents. This sometimes gave a new lease of life to artists who had semi-retired or fallen out of favour with the public. Several

An early Mac computer

collections of rare tracks and alternative takes by The Beatles called *Anthology 1, 2* and *3* were released mid-decade, and Eric Clapton had a hit with his album of acoustic recordings from the MTV show *Unplugged*. New albums were released by the re-formed Eagles (*Hell Freezes Over*, 1994) and later in the decade by Santana (*Supernatural*, 1999), and big-name artists from the 1980s had their careers extended into the 1990s with further albums (such as Sting with *Mercury Falling*, 1996, and U2 with *Pop*, 1997). One particular track that is worth listening to on Sting's *Mercury Falling* is 'I Hung My Head'. The disconcerting narrative is enhanced by the timing of nine quavers in a bar, which divide not into three lots of three, but into four plus five, so that the music is constantly unsettling.

CELTIC FUSION

Bodhrán: Irish hand-held drum. One hand holds the frame inside, where it can control the tension and pitch of the drumhead while the other uses a double-headed beater called a tipper.

The Celtic fusion genre, which had developed in the 1980s (see p. 93), had continued success in the early years of the decade, with its world music instrumentation and escapist subject matter finding popular appeal. Sinéad O'Connor had a huge hit with a cover of Prince's 'Nothing Compares 2 U' in 1990, and Enya, now a solo artist after leaving the band Clannad, had success with the album *Shepherd Moons* (1991). The single 'Caribbean Blue' from the album featured a mellow sound with warm vocals and synthesiser pads, creating a lilting New Age atmosphere in triple time. The Irish band The Corrs had commercial success, which built up during the decade towards their hit album *Talk on Corners* (1997). Their pop-orientated songs were infused with Irish fiddle music and **bodhrán** drumming to produce a stylistic integration.

The Corrs

GRUNGE ROCK

One area of the USA where the counter-cultural reaction to commercialism was evident was in the northwest city of Seattle. Here several bands were interested in back-to-basics post-punk values and rejected the polished visuals of MTV. This applied not just to their music but to their whole image; they appeared on stage wearing scruffy clothes and avoiding theatrical presentation such as complex light shows. This genre included groups such as Nirvana, Pearl Jam and The Smashing Pumpkins, who are credited as launching the alternative rock genre, and the style of their music is known as grunge.

MUSICAL EXAMPLE

NIRVANA, 'SMELLS LIKE TEEN SPIRIT' (1991)

This song is the most well-known track from the band's highly successful second album *Nevermind*. Features of the music include extreme dynamic contrast, a medium tempo and an F minor key, plus short melodic and harmonic patterns that run through the song, providing unity. The production ensures that Kurt Cobain's vocals can be heard clearly despite the heavily distorted rhythm guitar sound, with relatively up-front drums maintaining the beat.

Nirvana

Conjunct: Moving up or down by step. The opposite is disjunct, where notes move in a jumpy or angular way.

The opening features a repeated two-bar series of power chords played by Cobain on an undistorted electric guitar:

 F B♭ | A♭ D♭ :‖

- the second bar left-hand position simply moving up two frets from the first bar (or right-hand position in the case of Kurt Cobain as he was a left-hand guitarist).

0:06 A powerful drums fill leads into

0:08 a heavily distorted rhythm guitar repeating the same series of chords, with the drums and bass reinforcing the driving dotted rhythm.

0:24 The rhythm guitar drops out suddenly, and the volume level lessens as the bass continues the harmonic progression, and the drums adopt a more regular quaver rock pattern. Cobain, on lead guitar, plays plaintive rising 4ths of C and F.

0:32 Vocals enter with a melody built from broken F minor triads and falling four-note scales.

0:49 After eight bars the melody becomes **conjunct** (less angular), dwelling on repeated A♭s to Gs on the word 'Hello' and its rhyming 'How low?', with the distorted rhythm guitar joining in. This is the first section of the song to use double-tracking on the vocals.

1:05 Eight bars later we launch into the chorus as the vocals rise an octave, and the harmonic pattern continues, returning to the dotted rhythm of the opening material.

1:30 A new section begins, for the first time using different harmonies, moving in blocks down and up the fretboard to produce parallel chromatic movement of open 5ths:

1:39 Verse 2 begins in the same quieter mood as verse 1 and leads to the second chorus.

2:50 A guitar solo forms the basis of the next section but it avoids the virtuoso runs beloved of the heavy metal fraternity. It uses a spacy flanged sound that repeats the melody line of the opening vocals.

3:33 Verse 3 begins, and leads to the final chorus, which leads out of the song with the last words ('a denial') repeated several times, and a final F minor chord, strengthened with amplifier feedback.

Other US bands were inspired by the espoused values of Nirvana despite Cobain's tragic suicide in 1994. Pearl Jam, also from Seattle, had success with *Ten* (1992) and *Vs.* (1993), and in California the band Green Day (*Dookie*, 1994, and *Insomniac*, 1995) owed much to punk, with their fast tempi. The Red Hot Chili Peppers added funk rhythms to the alternative rock style.

The US singer-songwriter Jeff Buckley worked with the record producer Andy Wallace, who had mixed Nirvana's *Nevermind* album. In 1993 he formed a band and in 1994 released his debut album *Grace*, the title track of which is looked at in detail below. Tragically, Buckley died by accidental drowning in 1997.

MUSICAL EXAMPLE

JEFF BUCKLEY, 'GRACE' (1994)

Jeff Buckley

The song is set in E minor but begins with the chromatic chords of Fm^7 and Gm^7 played on synthesiser, whilst the lead guitar uses semiquaver arpeggios and scale patterns around the harmony. This leads to a heavy chord of E minor enhanced by sonic feedback followed by

0:10 strong rhythmic D and Dsus^4 chords strummed by the guitars, which set the pace with bass and drums and lead to

0:25 the entry of the vocal part, which moves up and down mainly by step over parallel moving harmonies with chords of Em I F Em I E♭ I. This chromatic harmony continues, and at

0:48 Buckley's voice rises 'for my fading voice sings', and falls down with a long **melisma** on 'love'.

1:10 A chorus section begins on the words 'wait in the fire', with a long melisma on the fourth use of the word 'fire'.

1:29 A return of the opening intro material.

1:56 Verse 2.

2:41 Chorus 2.

2:59 A bridge section begins, featuring parallel harmonies followed by wordless vocalisations in multiple parts creating a rich texture.

3:41 A repeat of the intro, then verse 3 followed by a coda that features a flanged electric guitar.

The song is unique for its dark chromatic harmony and inventive textures.

Melisma: Where many notes are used for just one syllable. Music that uses this device is known as melismatic, and the opposite, where each note is assigned to a single syllable, is known as syllabic.

BRITPOP

In the UK music had taken a different route. Alternative rock in Britain was also guitar based and used independent labels for recording, but didn't embrace the US grunge style. A cleaner, less distorted sound was used, with its musical roots in the late 1960s sound of The Kinks and The Beatles. It became known as Britpop.

Blur took their inspiration from The Kinks, and their album *Modern Life Is Rubbish* (1993) was a critique of life in the 1990s, preferring to look back nostalgically to a bygone era. *Parklife* (1994) was a cynical reflection of the times, with a varied set of subjects from the weather forecast ('This Is A Low'), Grecian holidays ('Girls And Boys') and the mundane life of a door-to-door double-glazing salesman ('Parklife'). In this track there are long passages of spoken prose, which give a touch of the cockney working-class narrative to the song. Damon Albarn, the band's primary songwriter, was skilled at the use of non-conventional harmonies in his songs. Sometimes it is difficult, particularly in the verses, to decide the home key in a Blur song. For example, in the song 'Coffee & TV' (1999) the verse consists of:

B | Am E | G F | B♭ C♯ |

It was common in Blur's songs for guitarists to slide to a chord on the next fret, making a chromatic harmony. This can be seen in 'Country House' (1995), where the verse chords, in the key of A, are:

E | Bm | Bm | D | D/C♯ | C♯⁷ ||

In 1998 Albarn formed the virtual band Gorillaz jointly with the comic book artist Jamie Hewlett, which comprised animated characters functioning on the band's website, and in videos and cartoons, the music being contributed by a variety of personnel. Its first album took its name from the band and sold over seven million copies. Blur continued together for some years, although their members sometimes worked on projects with other artists, enriching their song-writing techniques by sharing ideas.

The Manchester band Oasis was another successful band that earned the label 'Britpop'. The music press at the time set them up as rivals of Blur, even though their music was quite different. The music of Oasis was composed mostly by Noel Gallagher and was influenced by the melodic phrasing of The Beatles and the rock and roll sensibilities of T.Rex or The Rolling Stones. As well as being part of the Britpop movement, Oasis can be thought of as alternative rock, embracing the back-to-basics approach of their US counterparts. Their songs sound equally impressive on an electric guitar in a stadium as on an acoustic guitar strummed in a teenager's bedroom — coupled with the easy chords in many of the numbers, this means they are eminently playable by amateur musicians, which fits the non-commercial convictions of these movements. Their album *Definitely (Maybe)* (1994) sold well in the USA and worldwide. The song 'Live Forever' was released as a single ahead of the album and became the group's first number-one hit.

MUSICAL EXAMPLE

OASIS, 'LIVE FOREVER' (1994)

The appeal of this song is in its deceptively simple melody line, artful yet memorable, the straightforward diatonic harmonies and instrumentation together with the boy-next-door directness of the lyrics and vocal performance.

Oasis

The song begins with a whistle and a drum beat with a quaver feel lasting four bars.

0:11 The vocals and guitar come in together. The melody line kicks off with a falling third for 'Maybe', and the first eight bars move mostly around B, A and G. Harmony chords of G, D, Am⁷, C and D are used, all playable in **1st position**. This section can be regarded as a chorus, although the link to the verse is seamless.

0:33 The next part is a verse, as the lyrics change the second time around. Here the vocals are set higher around E and D and have a more urgent feel as they repeat one-bar phrases, illustrating lyrics such as 'I want to live, I don't want to die'. At the eighth bar a climactic high B is reached for 'live forever' (the song hook), and the melody drops to a non-harmony note of E against the chord of F. After an extra bar extending this verse section to nine bars,

0:57 the music returns for a repeat chorus, followed by verse 2.

1:42 A guitar solo based over the chords of the chorus and verse continues the music using pentatonic patterns and leading back to

2:27 a repeat of the chorus and verse 1, which links to

3:06 a coda based around the high 'live forever' motif, which repeats six times. The song concludes with a long guitar solo and a held chord of A minor.

It could be argued that the opening section is not a chorus, and therefore the song is in simple verse form. This ambiguity is part of the song's originality.

First-wave Britpop bands included Pulp, Suede, Blur, Oasis and Supergrass. Their success, with the exception of Oasis, was confined mostly to Britain despite US tours. Liam Gallagher would sometimes use a guitar decorated with a Union Jack, and when 'Cool Britannia' was adopted by Tony Blair and the newly elected Labour Party in 1997 the Britpop style had reached its peak, beginning a decline shortly afterwards, although the genre's influence can be traced in successful bands such as The Verve, Radiohead and the Stereophonics.

In the second half of the decade alternative rock bands such as Radiohead were producing an altogether more progressive style of music. They achieved national success with their second album (*The Bends*, 1995) and international recognition with their third (*OK Computer*, 1997).

RADIOHEAD, 'PARANOID ANDROID' (1997)

This is the second track from the album *OK Computer* and it reflects a number of characteristics commonly found in the prog rock genre (see p. 55). It is moderately lengthy (6:23) and employs non-standard time signatures and some unusual instruments. The music can be divided into clear sections.

Other examples of highly sectionalised tracks include 'Happiness Is A Warm Gun' by The Beatles from their *White Album* (1968) and Queen's 'Bohemian Rhapsody' from *A Night at the Opera* (1975).

Radiohead

The song is in G minor and an acoustic guitar introduction begins with a Cm chord; in bar 4 the strange Gm⁶/E♮ is used, which is featured on a number of occasions in the verse.

0:17 The vocals enter, high pitched, rising from C to a high B♭ and down again over four bars. Two extra bars of accompaniment lead to a repeat of the phrase.

0:47 The verse continues with long held notes to the words 'What's that?' and the bass line descends, this time using the strange E♮ as a bass for an E⁷ chord. After a repeat of the verse to new lyrics, the E⁷ acts as chord V⁷ for

1:57 a new instrumental section in A minor featuring a guitar riff which moves to using the chords of C, A♭ and B♭ in $\frac{7}{8}$ time.

2:19 The vocals join in, returning to A minor and following the riff shape.

2:31 More $\frac{7}{8}$ music takes us to

2:42 a violent electric guitar stab, punctuating the more urgent vocals 'You don't remember'.

3:03 A heavy electric guitar solo screams over the $\frac{7}{8}$ patterns, and suddenly a held chord of F leads to

3:33 a quiet dreamy section based on descending chromatic lines, and after 24 bars the melody forms a lower counterpoint to more vocals at 5:05:

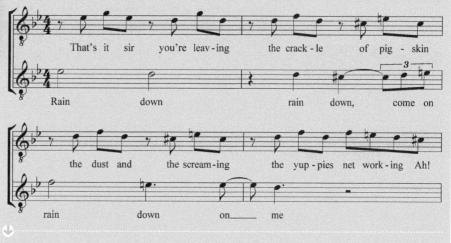

5:35 A return of the fast-moving A minor / C riff section concludes the song with a second guitar solo.

BOY BANDS AND GIRL BANDS

All-male singing and dancing groups had been around for some time, and bands from the 1960s such as The Osmonds or the Jackson 5 could be described as boy bands, particularly when their lead singers were teenagers such as Donny Osmond or Michael Jackson. In the 1990s there were a number of manufactured all-male groups that had a particular success, with their stage routines and videos targeting young girls in particular. The Irish group Boyzone and the British bands Take That and East 17 all had a series of hits in the UK. In the USA groups such as New Kids On The Block and New Edition enjoyed major success under the direction of Maurice Starr. Boyz II Men were targeted more towards adults, and in the second half of the 1990s the Backstreet Boys rose to prominence, although their initial breakthrough was in Europe.

MUSICAL EXAMPLE

TAKE THAT, 'EVERYTHING CHANGES' (1994)

The song was a single release from the 1993 album of the same name, and was written by their lead singer Gary Barlow. Both single and album reached number 1 in the UK charts. It is a dance track with a slow introduction, and is notable for its disco beat and jazz harmonies.

Take That

Modulate: To change key. This can be done gradually using a chord sequence or suddenly, in which case it is called an abrupt modulation.

Steel-strung acoustic guitar chords with a slight tremolo coupled with synth piano begin the music, playing F major 7th and C major 7th chords, creating a mellow jazz sound under a spoken lyric. Percussion cuts in with fast semiquavers and offbeat claps.

0:16 The music **modulates** to D major for the start of the singing and continues to employ major 7th chords. A high string melody introduces a two-bar hook that is destined to become chorus material later. The beat is now established with a four-on-the-floor sampled kick drum and a funky bass line.

0:31 Another key change to a major takes place for the verse proper. Despite the standard 16-bar length the musical phrases are designed to cover over any feeling of foursquare regularity. Note how the eighth bar contains a melody line where there would normally be a rest, and how many of the notes fall on quavers between the beats. Harmonies employ a number of minor 7th chords in the second half of the verse: C♯m⁷ F♯m I Bm⁷ I. Syncopations are emphasised by a piano sound and colour is added with glockenspiel notes, both played on synths.

1:00 Next comes the chorus, which is constructed from the two-bar hook from the start, sung by four of the five band members in unison, combined with material from the verse, which is taken by the lead vocal. Strings provide high harmonies and sometimes follow the vocal line.

1:45 The chorus repeats and then

2:16 a bridge section moves into C major using the harmonies from the introduction, which leads to a change back to D major for

2:30 a high tenor sax solo for eight bars and

2:46 repeated choruses, which fade the music out as the sax improvises against the vocal hook.

The all-girl group the Spice Girls became representative of the idea of 'Girl Power' under their manager Simon Fuller (see p. 121). The five girls put forward a list of instructions to their boyfriends in the song 'Wannabe' (1996), singing 'I'll tell you what I want, what I really really want', which contained a mixture of rap and close-harmony singing. It became a hit in 31 countries, and the biggest-selling single by a female act. They happily embraced the commercial side of pop, but in 1997 decided to run their affairs without a manager (and record sales declined as a result).

FEMALE ARTISTS IN CANADA AND THE USA

A number of female artists from Canada performed particularly successfully at this time, including the power ballad singer Celine Dion and the country rock superstar Shania Twain, the folksy singer-songwriter Sarah McLachlan and the rock-influenced Alanis Morissette.

In the USA teen idol acts such as Britney Spears and Christina Aguilera were enormously successful worldwide. Two female divas who fought for supremacy in the US charts were Whitney Houston and Mariah Carey. They both had very powerful voices and used a highly melismatic style of vocal technique influenced by soul. They were most at home with slow ballads where they could demonstrate their expressive interpretations.

Mariah Carey's first hit single was 'Vision Of Love' (1989), which is full of highly decorated vocal lines and became much imitated. The opening phrase sets the vocal style, with all the notes sung to the lyric 'Oh!'.

Mariah Carey

A fruitful comparison can be made between two cover versions of the song 'Without You'. If Mariah Carey's 1994 version is compared with Harry Nilsson's expressive yet straightforward interpretation, a good understanding of the Carey's melismatic vocal style can be obtained. Her hit single 'Hero', like many other ballads, is full of expressively shaped melismas. At the end of the first line of vocals, for example, she adds the following embellishment to what would ordinarily just be a movement from C♯ to B:

Whitney Houston had an equally expressive voice, as can be heard, for example, in the unaccompanied opening of the hit 'I Will Always Love You' (1992).

R&B

The type of singing discussed above had its roots in R&B and soul from earlier decades. At the end of the 1980s singers such as Tina Turner and Janet Jackson had dance hits that foreshadowed a type of black music that became known as contemporary R&B, which was slowed down to create soul ballads such as Janet Jackson's 'That's The Way Love Goes' (1993), Mary J. Blige's 'Not Gon' Cry' (1996) and Usher's 'Nice & Slow' (1998). The

Jimmy Jam and Terry Lewis: A US songwriting and production team that worked with a large number of R&B and other artists including The Human League, Michael and Janet Jackson, Boyz II Men, Usher, Mary J. Blige, Mariah Carey, Prince, Spice Girls, Vanessa Williams, George Michael, Melanie B and Rod Stewart. To date they have produced 17 number-one hits in the US Hot 100 charts. They are well known for their use of the Roland TR-808 drum machine.

contemporary R&B artists would also draw on hip-hop rhythms, samples and rap in their songs, and employ the slick production techniques of **Jimmy Jam and Terry Lewis**. Multiple-voiced textures were frequently employed and cleverly edited.

HIP HOP

The Fugees took hip hop to a new level in 1996 with their hit album *The Score*, with its use of melodic vocal samples and warm sound. Their lead singer, Lauryn Hill, left them shortly afterwards, and her solo album *The Miseducation of Lauryn Hill* (1998) features a variety of styles including reggae, R&B and soul.

MUSICAL EXAMPLE

LAURYN HILL, 'DOO WOP (THAT THING)' (1998)

The song consists of a rap verse and a sung chorus. The chorus features multiple layers of Hill's voice as she provides a duet texture which is combined with conversations among groups of both sexes. In the promotional video she uses a split screen; on the left she is set in the 1960s, with appropriate hairstyle and dress, and on the right she is in an up-to-date scene of the late 1990s.

Lauryn Hill with the Fugees

The music begins with high repeated piano chords alternating between Am and Gm each bar, under which vocal-backing triadic chords move up and down together with spoken dialogue.

0:19 Brass chords enter with a syncopated rhythm for four bars. The chords are in fact sampled and appear in other unexpected places in the song.

0:28 The piano returns with a sparse funk bass and Hill's rap verse. The lyrics are intended to encourage self-respect among the African-American female community. Various male and female spoken comments take place in the background.

0:48 Three sections of rap follow, with the bass becoming even funkier in the third under the high piano chords:

1:06 Brass chords return, leading to

1:35 a sung chorus part. accompanied by the same music as the verse. The second half features a falling fourth, emphasising 'that thing'.

1:55 A second verse begins, once again in rhythmical spoken rap, this time reduced from 24 bars to 16, followed by

2:33 four bars of brass chords, leading to

2:43 an a cappella section where the bass and piano drop out and multiple voices form a complex weaving texture held together by a deep male 'boom, boom' (perhaps a reference to the original doo-wop genre).

3:02 The sung chorus returns, is repeated and fades out.

3:58 This is not quite the end. Music and conversation are faded back in again for over a minute before the track finally ends.

The hip-hop style had never really taken off in the UK, remaining largely underground in the first half of the decade. Legal troubles around the licensing of samples dogged the early groups, although imaginative groups such as the London-based Stereo MCs, its members both talented musicians and producers, took to sampling their own music. Their 1990 album *Supernatural* contained the first ever British hip-hop single to reach the US charts ('Elevate My Mind'). The follow-up album released in 1992 used more live musicians, including a group of black female singers led by the UK soul diva Mica Paris. The title track 'Connected' was an international hit.

The commercial success of rap music in the late 1980s – artists such as De La Soul, Run-DMC and Queen Latifah – continued into the 1990s and became one of pop music's dominant styles, broadening its subject matter and fusing with mainstream music genres that previously were self-contained. It was even an influence on the music listened to by young people of white middle-class backgrounds. Some artists employed controversial subject-matter in their rap records, with aggressive lyrics and political commentary, often reflecting the concerns of the black community. Despite their overt criticism of the US media, Public Enemy had a mainstream breakthrough with their album *Apocalypse 91 . . . The Enemy Strikes Black* (1991), reaching number 4 in the charts, and artists such as N.W.A. used a style that became known as gangsta rap because of its themes of urban crime.

A rivalry between southern Californian and New York rap artists grew up. On the west coast artists such as Dr Dre and Snoop Doggy Dogg were particularly inventive with their rhyme patterns, creating interesting cross-rhythms against the backing tracks. Cypress Hill brought in a Latin flavour to their hip-hop records (*Black Sunday*, 1993). On the east coast in New York P. Diddy (aka Puff Daddy) formed his own record label (Bad Boy), and among its first crossover success was the Notorious B.I.G.'s *Ready to Die* (1994). Notorious B.I.G. (Christopher Wallace) was murdered in Los Angeles in March 1997, and as a reaction to this Puff Daddy recorded the concept album *No Way Out*. The single 'I'll Be Missing You' became an international hit, sampling the backing of The Police's single 'Every Breath You Take' and superimposing Faith Evans' vocals. The album version is preceded by speech over a sung version of the melancholic *Adagio for Strings* by Samuel Barber (to the words of the latin hymn Agnus Dei).

TRIP HOP

One particular subgenre derived from hip hop was uniquely British and was so successful that its style was exported back across the Atlantic. In the St Pauls area of Bristol in the late 1980s a group of DJs known as The Wild Bunch started playing slower music using Jamaican soundsystem practices. Three of their members formed a band named Massive Attack, and in 1991 released their first album *Blue Lines*. They pioneered a style that became known as trip hop in which, although it still utilised the looping breakbeats of hip hop, percussion samples were delivered at a slower pace with a deeper sonority; the music often sampled Rhodes pianos, trumpets and flutes. Other artists typical of the style include Portishead and Morcheeba.

**MASSIVE ATTACK,
'UNFINISHED SYMPATHY'
(1991)**

The track begins with a thudding heartbeat on the kick drum and some spacy effects. After a few seconds the breakbeat sample sets off at a medium tempo.

0:08   An open 5th, D to A, low down on strings, provides a harmonic context. A series of rich but dark string chords follow: Dm^7 I Dm^7 I F I Gsus^2 :ll

0:33   A soulful female voice set in the alto range begins the song; 11 bars of two- and one-bar phrases lead to a sudden octave rise, and the vocals soar up to a high F.

1:00   The music continues with the same dark string chords and sampled drum loop.

1:15   A repeat of the vocal verse begins with new lyrics, revealing the music as a love song.

1:41   After a repeat of the string interlude a new shorter section of reverberant vocals leads to

2:07   more string chords, with low piano notes emphasising the harmonic changes and some single, high piano notes setting points of light in a dark sky.

3:16   After more vocals the strings seem to take over. Dark discordant notes appear in the higher string register. There had always been a few deeper string discords as the track had progressed, but these move faster and are more strident, rising higher and becoming off the beat and highly discordant.

4:06   The discordant bubble bursts, and gentle tolling piano notes with quaver accompaniment lead to a final chord.

CLUB DANCE

The dance scene had taken something of a drop in popularity in the 1980s, particularly in the USA, as disco music became very unfashionable, and rock and country genres took on a new lease of life. In the UK the popular Wigan Casino Club had closed back in 1981, and northern soul was only kept going by CD re-issues. However, dance music continued. Underground clubs in Detroit and Chicago were producing a type of dance music known as techno, and by 1988 acid house had exploded in the UK. Abandoned warehouses in industrial areas were used for free parties, where house music was played, and on the holiday island of Ibiza the disco clubs played the new electronically created dance tracks. Nightclubs in the north of England – particularly in Manchester, Leeds and Sheffield – became more successful. In the 1990s mass parties, known as raves, were springing up, often unlicensed, with use of the euphoric drug ecstacy (MDMA) prevalent. The band Orbital took its name from the M25 motorway, which was used to link up raves on the outskirts of London. When the government of the day brought in legislation to stop the spread of raves in 1994, superclubs such as the Ministry of Sound in London and Cream in Liverpool sprang up, not just playing music but also producing compilation albums and other merchandise. These clubs also helped to fuel the concept of DJs as artists in their own right, for example Judge Jules, Paul Oakenfold and Sasha.

A bewildering selection of electronic dance subgenres developed during the late 1980s in the USA and the early 1990s in the UK. The table below is an attempt to describe the styles of some of the main ones, although there are many overlaps or crossovers in the descriptions. All are intended for dancing except chill out and ambient, with some drum 'n' bass albums intended for listening – for example Goldie's *Timeless* (1995), which blends jungle with symphonic strings and female vocals.

Style	Tempo (bpm)	Description	Example
Techno	120–150	Pumping bass lines, completely electronic and very regular.	Orbital, 'Desert Storm' (1991)
House	118–135	Synths and samples such as bongo loops or guitars.	Eve Gallagher, 'You Can Have It All' (1995)
Trance	130–145	Repeated synthesiser phrases that build up or break down during track with contrasts in dynamics. Rapid arpeggios and harsh gating. Central melodic hook.	Li Kwan, 'Point Zero' (1994)
UK garage	120–137	Syncopated drums, pitch shifted or chopped vocal samples, but danceable	M.J. Cole, 'Sincere' (1998)
Jungle/drum 'n' bass	160–190	Features manipulated breakbeats.	Goldie, 'Angel' (1995)
Chill out	75–115	Mid-tempo music with pads and loops intended as a break for dancers.	Chicane, 'Offshore' (1996)
Ambient	Very slow	Atmospheric music concentrating on timbres.	Aphex Twin, 'Lichen' (1994)

MUSICAL EXAMPLE

PRODIGY, 'BREATHE' (1996)

Taken from the album *The Fat of the Land*, this track can best be described as a blend of hardcore techno with jungle and punk attitude.

It belongs to a subgenre known as big beat. The promo video includes nasty insects, rats and crocodiles, with vocalist Keith Flint adopting an even nastier persona in his aggressive performance, spiked hair and make-up. Drums are sampled, although used in a traditional way for most of the time (often a live drummer would be used on stage).

Keith Flint from The Prodigy

The prodigy were named after the famous Moog Prodigy synthesiser, and the track begins with a synth guitar sample playing a disconcerting riff in E♭ minor:

0:14 The riff continues as a heavy drum loop is added, beginning with a powerful snare fill. Various samples are added over this, including forwards and backwards vinyl scratching sounds.

0:57 The vocals enter as the bass moves to V, then down two semitones, finishing on the E♭ of the key (B♭ | A♮ A♭ | E♭ | E♭ II). The lyrics of 'Breathe the pressure, Come play my game, I'll test ya' are shouted in a confrontational way over this progression. Repeats of the four bars lead to the vocalist singing the lyrics following the root notes.

1:30 Further spacy samples lead to a steel-strung acoustic guitar sample that is repeated, leading back to the home key, E♭, and then on to

2:01 verse 2 and a return of the opening riff and scratchy samples.

3:00 Verse 3 leads to a quieter passage, which gradually builds over a bass E♭ loop.

3:30 The build-up breaks up and leads back to

4:21 the opening riff and a return of the verse.

The Chemical Brothers were pioneers of the big beat style with their techno techniques and heavy breakbeats. Their 1996 single 'Setting Sun', which samples the voice of Noel Gallagher from Oasis, reached number 1 on both sides of the Atlantic. They made extensive use of samples. For example, in their UK number-one 'Block Rockin' Beats' (1997) the drums are sampled from a US session drummer, the vocals from a US rapper, and the guitar riff that runs through the song from a track by the US jazz fusion band the Crusaders, 'The Well's Gone Dry' (1974). It is clear, however, that the band's music is their own, as these samples form only a starting point. The guitar sample has some notes rearranged and is considerably speeded up, then is used in a completely different way from the original.

Fat Boy Slim was a British DJ and record producer who was very inventive in the way he used samples to create new pieces of music. He had the ability of cleverly choosing samples that often were quite lengthy and blending them into a seamless musical composition to which he would add a powerful-sounding, processed breakbeat of looping percussion. The following is a brief summary of the singles from his 1998 number-one album *You've Come a Long Way, Baby*.

Track title	Selected samples used	Composition
'The Rockafeller Skank'	'Beat Girl Main Title' – John Barry 'Sliced Tomatoes' – Just Brothers 'Peter Gunn' – Art of Noise featuring Duane Eddy 'Vinyl Dogs Vibe' – Vinyl Dogs featuring Lord Finesse	Up-tempo dance with a winding-down section in the middle, which picks up again and speeds up as an imaginary DJ manipulates a turntable.
'Gangster Tripping'	'You Did It' – Ann Robinson 'Feel The Heartbeat' – The Treacherous Three 'It's Yours' – T La Rock / Jazzy Jay 'Entropy' – DJ Shadow 'The Turntablist Anthem' – X-Ecutioners 'Word Play' – X-Ecutioners	Robinson's funky brass backing track mixes with rap, which moves smoothly into a Latin mambo. The party atmosphere breaks up briefly with repeated fast samples.
'Praise You'	'Lucky Man' – Steve Miller Band 'Balance & Rehearsal' – Hoyt Axton and James B. Lansing Sound Inc. 'Fat Albert Theme' – Ed Fournier 'Take Yo' Praise' – Camille Yarbrough 'Running Back To Me' – Ruby 'It's A Small World' – Walt Disney Records Studio Group	After a lo-fi acoustic piano intro Camille Yarbrough's vocals begin, slightly speeded up but pitch maintained. The vowel from the last word 'should' is massively extended by looping to last three-quarters of a minute, under which a percussion loop begins. Sampled guitar starts a new feel, and then the harmony changes. A sudden break leads back to the opening music, and a fast repeated sample leads to a climactic finish.
'Right Here, Right Now'	'Ashes, The Rain and I' – James Gang	An atmospheric slow build-up representing man's evolution. After the title is delivered by a repeated spoken sample, a drumbeat kicks in and the build-up continues.
'Build It Up, Tear It Down'	'Feelin' So Good (S.K.O.O.B.Y. D.O.O.) – The Archies 'Tobacco Road' – Eric Burdon and War 'The Acid Test' – Leo Muller	An energetic dance track set at around 150bpm that keeps going all the way through, although all harmony instruments drop out near the end and we are left with drums and spoken clips.

An American equivalent of Fat Boy Slim with a club dance orientation was the artist Moby who came to fame in 1991 by adding a house drum track to the string orchestra part of the theme for the TV drama series *Twin Peaks*. In his 1999 album *Play* he licensed the various tracks to various films, adverts and TV shows and the album became a worldwide success.

MUSICAL EXAMPLE

MOBY, 'WHY DOES MY HEART FEEL SO BAD?' (1999)

Moby

 The song begins with Moby playing an introduction on solo piano with the chords Am, Em, G and D – a harmonic progression that is maintained for the verses.

0:19 The main vocal sample begins, taken from the tenor lead of the Shining Light Gospel Choir from a 1953 vinyl record, singing the words of the title, complete with background noise, which Moby deliberately kept to retain the character of the sound.

0:38 A hip-hop breakbeat sample enters (combined with a Roland TR-909 drum machine), together with bass and high string lines doubled by piano.

1:37 A second choir sample appears, this time a soulful female voice singing 'these open doors', which echoes as the song progresses in a call-and-response fashion. There is a change of harmony to C, which moves to Am and later to F, making interesting harmonic changes under the same vocal phrase.

2:16 The tenor sample returns for a second verse, this time echoed by a grunge version, created by re-sampling at a lower quality and passing through a high-pass filter (which removes some of its deeper warmth and lets the high sound pass through).

2:56 The beat stops, and after a moment's silence a vocal sample from the choir, treated with heavy reverb, appears with a sustained accompaniment.

3:15 A lead from the drums takes the music back to a regular beat, featuring the female vocal sample from earlier, which repeats until

3:57 the beat stops again and the tenor vocals are given a similar treatment to the female sample at 2:56, with sustained chords which conclude the track.

The imaginative use of synths and samples with simple diatonic harmonies to accompany the vocal samples makes for a highly effective and structured composition.

MUSICAL INSTRUMENT

THE COMPUTER MUSIC SEQUENCER

Advances in computer technology throughout the decade helped to make possible music software that was an enormous help to both musicians and producers (although as time went on the distinction between these two occupations grew less). In the late 1980s programs such as Creator, and its integrated notation capability Notator, were created for the Atari ST computer (still used by Fatboy Slim), which because of its integrated MIDI ports became a favourite platform. However, the IBM PC computer became more powerful during the 1990s, and MIDI interface connections relatively cheap. Music software for the Windows environment soon became available, with Cubase VST (Virtual Studio Technology) and the updated Notator Logic, with even the ability to record and sequence audio alongside MIDI and mix down the results to music CD.

Most sequencers became track-based, with simultaneous playback of different sounds either from a connected keyboard or multi-timbral synthesiser module. Music could be recorded by playing it in live (real time) or entering notes one at a time (step time), and the more expensive software could add simulated digital effects such as reverberation or delay. Computers made the music easily editable, like a word processor, and music could be duplicated or cut up and rearranged.

As processing power and memory increased through the decade, it was even possible to use virtual instruments, digital forms of real instruments or programmable synths in software supplied by the progam writers.

One package beloved of dance music composers was made by the Propellerhead company and called Rebirth or, later, Reason. This was a virtual studio complete with synths, samplers and drum machines, including the acid-house favourite bass-line synthesiser the Roland TB-303 and the Techno drum machine – the TR-909.

Apple Mac software writers also produced a moderately priced sequencer called Garageband, but other computer platforms such as the Amiga and Archimedes became obsolete. Development of the software has been such that, by 2012, complete electronic music compositions of a professional standard can be produced on a standard laptop.

Reason software

DEVELOPMENTS IN MUSIC TECHNOLOGY

- 1990 Korg Wavestation Synthesiser first made
- Early 1990s: rapid growth in digital mixer sales (Yamaha introduced DMP7 in 1987)
- 1994 Logic version 1.7 E-magic added audio recording to computer MIDI sequencers
- 1996 Steinberg's Cubase VST launched
- 1997 Propellerhead Rebirth launched
- 1997 first DVD players go on sale in the USA.

CHAPTER 7

The 2000s and beyond

BACKGROUND

There were signs in the 2000s that the divergence of musical genres that had characterised the previous decade was no longer taking place. Genres spring up, fuse together and are re-defined overnight, as the information technology age means that communication of new artists and styles is global and virtually instant. In 2008 the US rapper Jay-Z was a headline act at Glastonbury, a festival traditionally associated with rock bands. Hip-hop techniques were incorporated into many of the new styles, artists from different musical backgrounds worked together on projects that integrated their styles – such as the rapper Eminem working with R&B singer Rihanna in 'Love The Way You Lie' (2010) – and crossover releases appeared more frequently in the charts, with artists able to draw from multiple fan bases. The table on the next page lists some of these crossover tracks.

Artist	Genres	Album	Music
Limp Bizkit	Heavy rock, hip hop, grunge: making nu-metal	*Chocolate Starfish and the Hot Dog Flavored Water* (2000)	Rappers contribute to a well-produced rock metal album.
Daft Punk	Synthpop, house, techno: making electro pop	*Discovery* (2001)	The soundtrack of an animated film, using samples that have instruments added by the band.
Arcade Fire	Indie rock, baroque rock, art rock	*Neon Bible* (2007)	Use of large numbers of acoustic folk instruments.
The White Stripes	Post-punk, new wave: making garage rock	*Elephant* (2003)	Duo employing old-fashioned recording equipment (no computers) and back-to-basics musical communication.
Alicia Keys	R&B, classical piano, jazz	*Songs in A Minor* (2001)	Melismatic singing, cool laid-back piano figures and multiple vocals (note the piano cadenza three-quarters of the way through the track 'Girlfriend').
Norah Jones	Jazz, soul, country	*Come Away with Me* (2002)	Mellow, acoustic, late-night listening.

INDIE MUSIC

A large number of the independent labels (indies) that existed during the 1980s had gradually been taken over by the major labels throughout the 1990s, partly because of distribution problems for small companies. One advantage such labels had over the large corporations was the ability to respond quickly to changes in the public's perception of up-to-date trends. The internet provided a solution for bands that wanted to be independent of the main music industry, as social networking sites such as MySpace enabled amateur artists to promote their music and reach a wide audience. The White Stripes and The Strokes were among a number of bands that achieved their early success through the increasing power of the internet. Listening to music online became viable because of the invention of the MP3 format, which compressed music files to a smaller size, allowing them to be streamed more easily than the full-range audio used by CDs. They could even be quickly downloaded and stored on a computer or transferred to personal music players that used hard disks for storage (such as Apple's iPod, first introduced in 2001).

The music of the Arctic Monkeys was already well known by the time they played their first major gig at the 2,000-seater London Astoria in 2006 because of internet file-sharing. A local photographer named Mark Bull had been posting their demos online under the title *Beneath the Boardwalk* (the Boardwalk being a local pub where they had been playing), and their first album on the indie label Domino Records had to be released early. *Whatever People Say I Am, That's What I'm Not* (2006) became the fastest-selling debut album in UK chart history and went straight to number 1 in the charts, as did their next three album releases.

MUSICAL EXAMPLE

THE ARCTIC MONKEYS, 'BRIANSTORM' (2007)

This track is taken from their second studio album, *Favourite Worst Nightmare*.

Alex Turner from The Arctic Monkeys

❄

Dry: A sound that has no reverberation applied to it. In recording terms, when a large amount of reverb is added to a track it is described as being 'wet'.

This song is a driving 'stormy' track with an exciting drum beat of alternating high and floor tom toms, four crochet beats together on high hat and kick drum, and the snare drum on beats two and four, all running at high speed:

with overdriven electric guitars beginning with a tremulando F to D♭.

⬇

0:22 After 16 bars everything stops except one **dry** lead guitar for a one-bar riff in F minor, which when the band comes back in is developed to the following power chord version:

accompanied by a bass moving with the riff, and drums that have changed to a quaver rock rhythm.

⬇

0:37 After this is played four times the vocals enter, at first stating the lyrics in short phrases then moving in crotchet triplets over the repeated open-5th riff. At the halfway point of the verse a second guitar adds a continuous repeated crochet-triplet pattern, creating an even more complex texture.

⬇

1:00 After a 16-bar verse the fast semiquaver drums return and then

⬇

1:12 verse 2 repeats the music from verse 1, although a high lead guitar adds a countermelody above the second half of the vocals.

⬇

1:36 The music now leaves F minor harmony and emphasises C for a bridge to

⬇

1:47 an instrumental section of more powerful lead guitars producing a thick texture that is suddenly relieved by

⬇

2:10 verse 3, where for the first half all the guitars drop out and the vocals are accompanied only by pounding tom toms.

⬇

2:22 The second half of verse 3 is once again accompanied by the guitars, coming back in on the word 'Thunder' after a beautifully timed second of silence, leading to

⬇

2:34 the end of the verse and a sudden stop. But in fact it is another slightly longer silence, this time of two bars, and the music resumes with the guitars from the intro to finish with eight bars of pure energy.

The term 'indie' had, during the late 1980s, started to be used to describe a musical subgenre of alternative rock, not just a type of record label. It was usually associated with bands that attempted to maintain an underground perspective, drawing from styles used by garage rock and post-punk bands with their back-to-basics approach. By the 2000s there were many indie rock bands some becoming highly successful. UK examples include Bloc Party ('Two More Years', 2005), and the Kaiser Chiefs ('Ruby', 2007). The Kooks had some success reviving Britpop (*Inside In/Inside Out*, 2005) but although their style was indie rock they were signed to a major label (Virgin Records).

The Killers are a good example of an indie rock band from the USA, although their music sold particularly well worldwide; their debut album *Hot Fuss* (2004) reached number 1 in the UK charts and contained four tracks released as singles:

- 'Somebody Told Me': medium rock tempo in a minor key. The high bass melodic phrases in the introduction and the short melodic licks from the lead guitar in the verse are particularly effective. The catchy chorus begins after two strong accents on the first two beats of the bar and is constructed from short phrases that repeat while harmonies change underneath.

- 'Mr Brightside': the music sets off with an undulating guitar riff that runs through the verse. The notation below doesn't match the audio, as the guitars are tuned down a semitone to D♭.

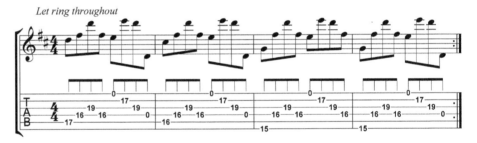

The verse is made up of quaver repeated Ds (D♭s) in one-bar lines of lyrics, but in contrast the chorus is more sustained.

- 'All These Things That I've Done': standard-length 16-bar verse with interesting syncopations derived from the lyrics. There follow two chorus sections, the first, to the words 'Help Me Out', is extended the second time it appears to 13 bars. The middle section is also like a chorus as it contains an important hook that invites everyone to join in with the repeated lyrics 'I got soul, but I'm not a soldier'.

- 'Smile Like You Mean It' begins with a soaring synthesiser line based on a rising 6th that appears both in the intro and throughout the chorus.

The Killers used melodic sing-along choruses and rocky rhythms that are reminiscent of Britpop, and it is unsurprising that the band were so successful in the UK with these characteristics.

BRITISH ALTERNATIVE ROCK

Two British alternative rock bands that were formed in the late 1990s but had their commercial breakthroughs with major labels in the 2000s were Coldplay and Muse. Coldplay had instant success with their first album, *Parachutes*, released on the Parlophone label in 2000, and its pre-release single 'Yellow' earned them worldwide recognition. They were influenced by post-Britpop bands such as Radiohead, Embrace ('My Weakness Is None Of Your Business', 1998) and the Scottish band Travis ('Turn', 1999), and mixed sensitive lyrics with a uniquely tuneful take on melody that combines with a more abrasive instrumentation. Their second album *A Rush of Blood to the Head* (2002) was also successful, winning the band several awards. One of the singles released from the album, 'Clocks', won record of the year in 2004.

MUSICAL EXAMPLE

COLDPLAY, 'CLOCKS' (2003)

Chris Martin from Coldplay

Root: The bottom note of a chord.

The music for this track is based around a repeated piano ostinato running at 130bpm that has a hypnotic effect. It is reminiscent of pieces by the 'classical' minimalist composers such as John Adams or Steve Reich, apart from its rock-band instrumentation.

0:15   After eight bars of piano and synth pad chords, the bass enters playing repeated-quaver **root** notes. Drums also use the quaver rhythm, with snare accents on the top notes of the piano riff on beats 1, 2½ and 4.

0:29   Vocals enter with a four-bar descending phrase and the piano drops out, although the harmonies derived from the piano riff are still there together with the snare accents. The four-bar phrase is repeated four times until

0:59   the vocals move to a high falsetto range, where they become more sustained for the words 'You are', which repeats.

1:13   The piano ostinato re-enters over the repeated harmonies for an eight-bar link to take the music back for

1:28   verse 2, complete with the higher sustained section.

2:26   Now the piano ostinato pattern changes slightly, introducing non-harmony notes, although the sustained chords and bass stay the same.

2:56   After more high vocals the harmonies now change, with a move to a key a tone lower (D♭) and beginning with a G♭maj⁷ chord. This new harmony lasts for 13 bars until

3:25   the original piano pattern from the intro returns, and a coda completes the song with the vocalist wanting to return home.

Muse are similar to Coldplay in their musical originality but prefer a bigger sound with heavy percussion, driving electric guitars and multiple studio overdubs. Despite only numbering three players they are known for their powerful live performances; the lyrics of their songs deal with ambitious sci-fi or apocalyptic themes. They are highly able performers and their music often employs additional instruments such as the pipe organ and Mellotron used on the band's second album (*Origin of Symmetry*, 2001) or the string ensembles found on their third album (*Absolution*, 2003).

Matthew Bellamy from Muse

In Muse's album *Absolution* Matthew Bellamy (lead vocals, guitar and keyboards) shows the influence of classical composers such as Rachmaninov in his piano playing. In the epic track 'Butterflies And Hurricanes' he produces a piano cadenza that sounds as if it is from a Romantic concerto. The track 'Hysteria', from the same album, demonstrates the band's favourite technique of using a heavy bass guitar riff to propel the music forwards. The fast semiquaver bass riff in 'Hysteria' is joined by a lead guitar counterpoint after the second verse.

In their 2006 album *Black Holes and Revelations* Muse took a turn towards a more electronic sound. It was influenced by the 1980s synthpop of Depeche Mode, with Bellamy using arpeggiators and synthesisers, together with music from southern Italy and the Middle East. The more guitar-driven funk-rock track 'Supermassive Blackhole' was used in the 2008 teen-vampire film *Twilight*.

EMO

Another form of rock that was common at the start of the decade was called emo. It originated in the USA in the mid-1980s and was originally known as emotional hardcore, as it was characterised by a more melodic twist applied to a post-punk style. Emo is also a subculture and applies to the fashion and hairstyles of young white teenagers as well as to their music. Jimmy Eat World's hit single 'The Middle' from the album *Bleed American* (2001) is a well-known example of the style. Its simple, happy melody; straightforward harmonies of I, IV and V (D, G and A); and bouncy beat made it instant pop-hit material.

TELEVISION

Television played an important role in promoting new artists throughout the decade, not just by playing their music as on MTV but also by actually discovering them and helping them achieve record deals. MTV had diversified during the decade, and although it produced a number of sister channels broadcasting music its main focus was on reality shows that featured unscripted drama using ordinary people. This change was partially due to the challenge presented by internet music-video broadcasting. A number of reality

TV shows that aimed to give amateur performers a chance of commercial success, with lengthy talent contests running for several weeks, sprung up. These gradually eliminated contestants and even allowed viewing audiences to vote for their favourite acts. In 1999 the *Popstars* series, based in New Zealand, became the inspiration for the UK's *Pop Idol* show, produced on ITV and founded by the entrepreneurial artist-manager and media businessman Simon Fuller, the first series being won by Will Young. Fuller went on to create the *American Idol* show (first series won by Kelly Clarkson), but *Pop Idol* was replaced by *The X Factor* in 2004. Girls Aloud were the successful winners of *Pop Stars: The Rivals* but it wasn't necessary to win to achieve commercial success. The R&B singer Lamar only came third in the final of BBC's *Fame Academy*, but since has produced seven top-ten singles (including 'If There's Any Justice', 2004).

SOLO ARTISTS

The 2000s saw success for a number of singer-songwriters from the UK, some of which are shown below along with one of their hit albums and singles.

Artist	Album	Year	Single
Dido	*Life for Rent*	2003	'White Flag'
James Blunt	*Back to Bedlam*	2004	'You're Beautiful'
David Gray	*Life in Slow Motion*	2005	'The One I Love'
James Morrison	*Undiscovered*	2006	'You Give Me Something'
Amy MacDonald	*This Is the Life*	2007	'This Is The Life'
Adele	*19*	2008	'Chasing Pavements'

Some female solo artists from the UK that used composers to write their songs include Katie Melua (debut album *Call Off The Search*, 2003, with songs written by Mike Batt), the soul singer Amy Winehouse (debut album *Frank*, 2003, with Winehouse being involved in the composition of the songs) and Lily Allen (debut album *Alright, Still*, 2006), the latter producing her early success through posting a profile on MySpace and uploading some of her music, which she had composed by working collaboratively with several other US and Jamaican musicians.

Norah Jones is a US singer-songwriter and daughter of the famous sitar player Ravi Shankar. She was influenced by a variety of styles including country, jazz, soul and pop idioms, and often sings at the piano using a sensitive and economical keyboard technique. Her rich expressive voice and the generally slow to medium tempi she adopts make her songs very intimate and ideal for late-night listening.

MUSICAL EXAMPLE	
NORAH JONES, 'NOT TOO LATE' (2007)	A simple piano introduction using F, Dm and C chords – with single root notes in the left hand and triads in the right hand on the offbeats – serves to set the mellow tone of this song.

0:23   The vocals enter with a melody falling from A to middle C. This repeats three times and is extended into a longer phrase the last time to end on a low alto F and complete the balanced phrasing, ending on the open-sounding chord IVsus^2 (B$^\flat$sus^2 = B$^\flat$, C and F).

0:45   An extra octave below is added to the left hand as the second line of lyrics begins, which repeats the music with Jones supplying a more decorated soul version of the tune.

1:06   The harmony now changes to C Gm I B$^\flat$sus^2 I to accompany the title lyrics which repeats three times, the third time extended again to add the words 'for love'. On the recorded version subtle strings creep in during this section, but the entry of the pizzicato bass and brushed drum kit is clear enough at the end of verse 1. The song then returns to the opening music and links back to

1:34   verse 2, and an extension on the words 'for love' leads into

2:55   a piano instrumental section based around the opening harmonies. This uses Jones' usual sensitive dynamics with accents and acciaccaturas from the country music tradition. This closes the song gently with a slight rallentando and perfect cadence.

Successful bands from the 1990s saw some of their members breakout with solo careers in the 2000s, some of them highly successful. Robbie Williams left Take That, Justin Timberlake did well after being in the boy band 'N Sync, and Beyoncé Knowles from Destiny's Child became a star on her own. All used professional management and production practices, as did the teen popstars that flooded the charts during the early 2000s, such as Britney Spears ('… Baby One More Time', 1999), Christina Aguilera ('Come On Over Baby (All I Want Is You), 2000) and Avril Lavigne ('Complicated', 2002).

CONTEMPORARY R&B

The teen popstars' successful formula was eclipsed shortly after by a dramatic rise in the popularity of contemporary R&B, which had incorporated elements of hip hop into its musical language. The blending of the two styles had been taking place since the late 1980s with the music known as new jack swing, and during the 1990s with hip hop soul, which replaced synthesisers with samples. In the 2000s the more rhythmical and smoother sound of contemporary R&B began to favour more solo artists than groups. Leaders in this style included Jennifer Lopez, Rihanna, Beyoncé Knowles, Mary J. Blige, Joss Stone, Mariah Carey, Alicia Keys and Jennifer Hudson. Male singers who adopted the new R&B style included Justin Timberlake, Usher, R. Kelly and Chris Brown, but it was the female performers that had the greatest commercial success.

MUSICAL EXAMPLE

BEYONCÉ KNOWLES, 'CRAZY IN LOVE' (2003)

Beyoncé combined her background of soul and R&B singing in Destiny's Child with a number of hip-hop artists and rappers such as Jay-Z, Sean Paul, Big Boi and Missy Elliot for her first solo album *Dangerously in Love*. The opening track, 'Crazy In Love', uses Jay-Z (later to become her husband) to start the song.

Destiny's Child. Beyoncé is far right.

Jay-Z comments over a repeated brass section sampled from a song by the 1970s group the Chi-Lites called 'Are You My Woman?'

0:14 The backing stops although the drumbeat continues while Beyoncé begins a rhythmical 'Uh Oh' based on a descending fourth of D to A. After two more bars of brass sample,

0:29 Beyoncé begins the song with eight bars of rhythmical vocalisations moving only by step, progressing to

0:48 a chorus based on the lyrics 'Got me looking so crazy right now', based on a one-bar phrase repeating eight times, with the last two joined by backing vocals in close harmony and a regular-quaver bass line of root notes.

1:07 Four bars of 'Uh oh's lead to

1:17 a repeat of the verse to new lyrics and a chorus, leading to

2:00 a stop verse rapped by Jay-Z with Beyoncé contributing background textures.

2:44 A bridge begins with vocals and accompaniment but ends with drums and harmony vocals, leading to

3:08 a repeated chorus and fade out.

The song has a busy texture of background soul vocals, samples and instruments that contribute towards the hectic party atmosphere that was part of the R&B idiom.

Usher's musical style derives from the soul vocals, jazz harmonies and funky rhythms of Stevie Wonder. His good looks, dancing skills and melodic R&B tracks made him a best-selling artist of the 1990s and 2000s.

MUSICAL EXAMPLE

USHER, 'U REMIND ME' (2001)

The song is a relaxed medium-tempo ballad in the key of E♭ minor. The sultry atmosphere is created though the use of the key's minor 7th chord and a repeated harmonic progression of E♭m⁷ | A♭m⁷ B♭m⁷ :‖

Usher

The four-bar introduction uses light strings with a descending woodwind motif that keeps going during the verse. This motif is destined to become the main hook of the chorus.

0:10 A sampled drum loop kicks in at the start of the verse, during which Usher sings a rising and falling melody based on two-bar phrases, with a rising perfect 5th contributing to its tunefulness.

0:31 The verse repeats with the vocals becoming more soul-like and melismatic (see the word 'do' in bar 4):

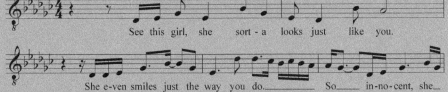

Verse 2

See this girl, she sort - a looks just like you.

She e-ven smiles just the way you do._____ So____ in-no-cent, she__

0:51 A chorus sung in close parallel harmonies that gradually change with Usher's overdubbed vocals creates a more and more complex texture of soulful polyphony.

1:12 The music returns for verse 3 and another chorus, and then moves on to a

1:52 bridge section, with new harmonies introducing V⁷ for the first time and Usher's vocals sounding even more like Stevie Wonder. The bridge leads to

2:12 a pause in the beat on a held chord of D♭/E♭ while Usher launches into a long descending vocal melisma.

2:23 The chorus returns while Usher improvises melodic phrases above the texture.

The chorus repeats five times, with the third time omitting the drums and the last dropping the backing out gradually to leave Usher to sing the last line unaccompanied.

Usher's single 'Yeah' from his 2004 album *Confessions* became a worldwide number-one hit. The song is deceptively simple with a short synthesiser riff running through:

Above this, Usher and his backing vocals create a complex texture of speech and song against a simple drum pattern and offbeat handclaps. It is remarkable for its lack of harmony instruments and bass line.

One of the most successful R&B singers of the decade was Rihanna, who as of 2011 has sold 60 million singles worldwide. She originated in Barbados and moved to the USA at the age of 16, where she signed to Def Jam Recordings. Her third studio album spawned four chart-topping singles, including 'Take A Bow'.

MUSICAL EXAMPLE	
RIHANNA, 'TAKE A BOW' (2008)	Rihanna's rich contralto voice appears at the start of the song as part of an eight-bar introduction. The melody centres around the key note E but increases its range with each phrase – the first phrase a semitone, the second phrase a 3rd, and the third phrase a 5th, characterised by an expressive melisma. The accompaniment is relatively light, with the piano playing rising quaver arpeggios combined with a sampled drum loop featuring synth handclaps. The last chord is based on the flattened 7th of the key (D♮), and the quaver movement stops as the chord is held. This harmonic device is to feature at the end of phrases throughout the music.

0:24   The main song begins with a falling motif that spans an octave down to a low G♯. The harmony uses the progression E B I C♯m A :ll which repeats, making a total of four phrases, with the last holding the D♮ chord mentioned above.

0:48   A new section begins based on two lots of two-bar phrases, and ending on the D♮ again, but the music moves on to

0:59   single-bar phrases that act as a kind of chorus hook and end with the first significant change in the repeated harmonies, with an F♯m for 'but it's over now'. Other differences in this section include crotchet instead of quaver movement, giving more rhythmic emphasis, and the inclusion of backing singers. A soul-like melisma leads into

1:29   verse 2, which continues to use the backing singers.

2:32   A section based on B harmonies acts as a bridge, using rising syncopated vocals that lead to

2:56   a return to the first bars of the introduction, cut short to four bars and jumping to

3:09   the chorus-like material, with a fuller string accompaniment which is used for a climax. This leads to

3:37   a short two-bar coda that ends the song on chord IV, using the words 'but it's over now'.

The song is deceptively simple with subtle phrasing and melodic hooks that avoid the obvious and are expressively delivered by Rihanna's soulful voice.

HIP HOP

Hip-hop styles had developed further through the 1990s and early 2000s with more capable technology and the replacement of the DJ record decks by samplers and computer mixing (although turntablism and scratching techniques continued to be practised away from the mainstream). Hits such as DJ Shadow's 'Six Days' (2002) made extensive use of samples to create new compositions – in this case including the vocal line from the British band Colonel Bagshot's 'Six Day War' (1971). DJ Shadow's debut studio album *Introducing* (1996) was the first to be made completely from samples. He used relatively modest equipment for this – an Akai MPC60 mkII sampler, twin turntables and Pro-tools software. The US record producer Kanye West used Curtis Mayfield's brass section from his funk track 'Move On Up' (1971) and slowed it down from 140bpm to 105bpm while he provided a rap commentary over it. The progress of the track is suddenly interrupted by a spoken section based on an interview and an argument, and when the music resumes the brass sample starts at full speed but quickly slows down back to its processed tempo.

Kanye West's single 'Gold Digger', which featured the vocals of Jamie Foxx, was remarkable for its 80,000 digital downloads in a week – a record at the time.

MUSICAL EXAMPLE

KANYE WEST (FEAT. JAMIE FOXX), 'GOLD DIGGER' (2005)

Kanye West and Jamie Foxx

Anacrusis: The upbeat, or unaccented notes at the beginning of a phrase before the accented downbeat (which comes at the beginning of a bar).

■ The music starts with the unaccompanied vocals of Jaime Foxx processed with digital delay and set high in the vocal range (moving lower as the phrase progresses). The melody is divided into one-bar phases, with a three-quaver **anacrusis**. When 6½ bars are completed a heavy kick drums enters with repeated semiquavers. Originally the melody was a sample of Ray Charles' voice but Foxx (who played Charles in the 2004 film 'Ray') was employed for Gold Digger.

0:17 The vocal sample repeats in the background as West begins his rap, which concentrates on the subject of a man who is manipulated by a woman seeking financial gain. The first set of lyrics against the singing acts as a chorus. The kick drum continues underneath with a syncopated two-bar semiquaver rhythm created by missing out the third beat of bar 1 and the second half of bar 2. Strong sampled handclaps are used on beats 2 and 4, along with scratching produced by New York DJ A-Trak.

1:18 The rap chorus repeats.

1:39 Verse 2 of the rap begins.

2:10 At this point there are spoken repeats of West's lyrics by male rappers. There have, however, been various spoken echoes as the track has progressed.

2:21 A repeat of the chorus lyrics.

2:41 Verse 3 of the rap with rhythmic pulse-wave synthesiser sounds.

3:12 The second half of the chorus lyrics conclude the song, with additional electronic effects.

The effectiveness of the song is due to a combination of West's lyrics and delivery, the Foxx vocals – which repeat throughout and are easily identifiable, starting at their high pitch – and the hip-hop drum beat and samples from various artists.

The hip-hop rapper and record producer Eminem has sold 33 million track downloads and 39.6 million albums in the USA alone. His use of dense rhyme patterns marks him out as an expert rap performer. The lyrics below are taken from the first verse of 'Sing For The Moment' from his album *The Eminem Show* (2002):

> These ideas are nightmares for white parents
> Whose worst fear is a child with dyed hair and who likes earrings
> Like whatever they say has no bearing
> Its so scary in a house that allows no swearing
> To see him walking around with his headphones blaring
> Alone in his own zone, cold and he don't care

His third album *The Marshall Mathers LP* (2000) is highly thought of and features subject matter that is very personal, dealing with the artist's childhood and family, his wife and his rise to stardom. The most successful single released from the album was 'Stan', which is a narrative concerning the suicide of an imaginary fan and features a sample of the first two lines of Dido's song 'Thank You' (2001), which unusually became a hit after the release of the song that sampled it.

MUSICAL EXAMPLE	
EMINEM, 'STAN' (2000)	

The track begins with thunder and lightning sound effects and a sample of Dido singing the verse of 'Thank You', rendered in lo-fi as if playing as part of the story (**diegetic**).

0:24   The full sound of the sample takes over (non-diegetic), leading to

0:48   the spoken words of Stan as he writes his fan letter.

1:36   The track continues with alternating sections between Stan's speech and the Dido sample with more sound effects including thunder, the sound of the pencil scratching on the letter paper, a car breaking and a news reporter.

3:36   In the third section of Stan's spoken narrative his delivery becomes more agitated as he struggles with drugs and alcohol. In the background faint screams from his wife lead to sound effects of screeching brakes and splashing sounds as the car is driven off the bridge.

5:24   The fourth section of speech concerns Eminem writing a letter in reply to Stan's fateful effort.

Diegetic: Sound that is part of the narrative of a film or video and so can be heard by its characters, rather than background music only heard by the viewer.

Auto-tune: A digital processor that was originally designed to correct vocal parts that were sung out of tune. Some producers used the effect for more creative purposes, by setting its controls so that the end result is a vocal line that seems to move in steps like the notes on a keyboard. Famous examples of this are Cher's disco hit 'Believe' (1998) and Janet Jackson's funky dance number 'All For You' (2001). Modern units such as the Antares AVP1 are also capable of rhythmic correction and adding effects to the sound of the vocal line such as compression (squeezing the peaks and troughs), EQ (adjusting the tone quality) de-essing (taking out unwanted vocal hissing) and double-tracking, as well as emulating various microphone models.

One of the most successful hip hop bands of the decade was The Black Eyed Peas, made up of three rappers and a female singer. Their third album *Elephunk* (2003) deliberately adopted a polished pop sound designed to attract mass audiences, with tracks like 'Shut Up' and 'Hey Mama' having a very danceable beat. Other dance-orientated songs were released as singles from their 2009 album *The E.N.D.*, such as 'Boom Boom Pow', which utilised the **auto-tune** processing effect on its vocals, and 'Rock Your Body', with its accompanying cyborg video, both tracks reflecting the more electronic sound of the album.

MUSICAL EXAMPLE

THE BLACK EYED PEAS, 'IMMA BE' (2010)

The album *The E.N.D.* is accompanied by many futuristic sci-fi videos based on technological cyborgs and heavy weapons. In 'Imma Be' the band is chased by a tall monster robot.

Some military-sounding snare drum beats frame a vocal sample of 'Imma Be', which is rhythmically repeated against a wooden click, all forming a ten-bar introduction.

0:25 Fergie, the lead female singer, begins the vocals unusually with a rap accompanied by more 'Imma be' samples and a syncopated kick drum.

1:05 The military snare marks the start of a second verse taken by Will.i.am one of the three male rappers. The rap is divided into sections by the snare drum fill.

2:09 After another snare drum marker a section begins which includes high sung notes. It builds up to faster music with a regular drum beat and rising vocal lines to the words 'Imma be, livin' that good life'.

2:28 A forward-moving section with a four-on-the floor kick drum, growling bass synth licks and offbeat handclaps.

3:32 Accented 'heys' on the eigth or last quaver of the bar are combined with the vocals of the rapper apl.de.ap.

4:10 The song finishes with everyone singing 'Imma be' unaccompanied.

The band's use of rhythms, tempi and samples produces a highly effective composition, like most of the tracks on this best-selling album.

The UK band The Streets produced a form of rap that didn't copy US accents but rather delivered their rhyming spoken lyrics with a blend of West Midlands and London dialect. Their music used a mixture of guitar and keyboards, with Mike Skinner rapping in the verses, synth and sample instrument licks, and sung pop hooks for the choruses (for example 'Fit But You Know It' from the 2004 album *A Grand Don't Come for Free*).

DANCE MUSIC

There had been important developments in UK dance music during the 1990s. UK garage (see p. 109), a form of electronic dance music descended from Chicago house styles, developed in parallel with jungle into speed garage and 2-step garage, with faster tempi and avoidance of the bass drum four-on-the-floor. The 2-step style featured rapped vocals, syncopated synthesiser bass lines, and snare and woodblocks accents in unusual places with use of triplets; sampled rhythm and melody instruments were sometimes used to give colour. The style reached its peak at the end of the decade with artists such as Artful Dodger ('Re-Rewind (The Crowd Say Bo Selecta)', 1999). A more stripped-down version of 2-step developed in the early 2000s into a subgenre known as grime, which was a fast 2-step groove (140bpm), employing futuristic electronic sounds with deep and harsh bass lines. Leading artists included Dizzee Rascal ('Fix Up, Look Sharp', 2003) and Wiley ('Wot Do U Call It', 2004), who achieved international recognition. Many young artists, though, found it difficult to achieve record deals at first and used the internet to promote their music (now mostly through Facebook's social networking and YouTube's video-sharing, sites that had to some extent taken over the role of MySpace).

In common with grime and the Sheffield-based bassline subgenres, a popular form of UK dance music known as dubstep also featured the use of a deep bass and was usually instrumental. Its characteristics are set out below.

Characteristic	Description
Bass	Deep sub-bass sound, utilising the large bass sub-woofer speakers found in clubs. Avoids the four-on-the-floor of traditional house and instead uses syncopated but sparse short phrases. Sometimes synthesiser editing produces a 'wobble' on a held note using LFOs or filter cut-offs (see p. 58).
Rhythm	Syncopated overlaid samples using shuffled patterns or triplets and cross-rhythms; 138–142bpm. Sometimes utilises the half-step pattern with only one snare strike per bar and lazy offbeat kick drum beats. High hat shuffled rhythms are prominent, as are claps. The deep kick drum interacts with the synth bass (sometimes achieved by using 'ducking'). Percussion sometimes will pause for a bar creating a break called a bass drop.
Harmony	Minor keys often used for a dark sound.
Melody	Sometimes angular-shaped riffs with awkward intervals such as an augmented 4th (tritone). Lead lines less likely to be spatial.
Production	Spatial atmospheres with echo, reverb (particularly on the snare drum and synth pads) and panoramic stereo. Use of pitch shift.

Good examples of the genre include Burial (*Untrue*, 2007), Kryptic Minds (*One Of Us*, 2009), Skream ('Exothermic Reaction', 2011) and the more pop, dance-orientated Magnetic Man ('I Need Air', 2010) and Katy B ('Katy On A Mission', 2010).

MUSICAL EXAMPLE

KATY B, 'KATY ON A MISSION' (2010)

The song was co-written and produced by Benga, a dubstep music producer from Croydon, and is Katy B's debut single released from her 2010 album *On A Mission*.

Although dubstep is often instrumental, Katy B's R&B vocals are supported by a number of dubstep techniques, notably the sub-bass, synthesiser triplet rhythms and the key of C minor together with overall high levels of reverberation.

Canon: A compositional device which uses one or more imitations of a phrase, entering after a set time and creating overlaps.

Four lines of reverberated vocals with a short delay begin, in quavers, and are supported by synthesisers employing crotchet triplets.

0:18 The bass enters playing sustained deep notes in crotchet triplets while the vocals continue in two-part harmony.

0:32 The drums enter in a regular rhythm, with the bass drum playing dotted notes, the snare only appearing on beat 3 and high hats emphasising second-quaver beats. Vocal phrases are cut off by overdubbed vocals in a C, E♭, C, E♭, C quaver pattern.

0:42 A melodic chorus hook completes the phrasing.

0:59 This is repeated four times, and echoed by a heavily processed version laden with timed delay echoes set at a crotchet beat apart, creating a **canonic** effect. A sawtooth synth sound plays G to A♭ quavers underneath:

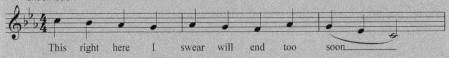

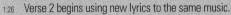

This   right   here   I   swear   will   end   too   soon

1:26 Verse 2 begins using new lyrics to the same music.

2:22 The echoed chorus also repeats, but this time using crotchet triplets in the accompaniment.

2:49 A short repeat of material from verse 2 leads to an instrumental finish.

Ellie Goulding

Many artists' songs have been remixed using dubstep techniques. Ellie Goulding had a chart success with her cover version of Elton John's 'Your Song' (2010), which significantly changed John's harmonies and gave the song a different flavour. However, the song was remixed in a dubstep style, which took it to a further level of inventiveness. A comparison between the original Elton John and Ellie Goulding's versions shows that Goulding avoids 7th chords and uses a four-chord pattern very different from the original, although she sticks more closely to the Elton John's near the end of the verse to help the turnaround. The dubstep version created by the Scottish producer Blackmill includes a very extended section at the end of the verse and leaves out the bass until this section is reached, where it makes a powerful entry.

Lyrics	It's a little bit funny	this feeling inside	I'm not one of those who can	easily hide
E John	I IVmaj⁷	V III	VI VI/Vbass	VI VI/♯VIbass
E Goulding	VI I	IV I	VI I	IV I III/VIIbass
Dubstep	Added drum beat with shuffling high hats			

I don't have much money but	boy, if I did	I'd buy a big house where	we both could live	
I V	III♯3/♯Vbass VI	I II⁷	IV V	V Vsus⁴ V
VI I	IV I	I II	IV V	V Vsus²
		Kick drum drops out		Extended reverbed section on 'big, big house', featuring synth triplet figure

LADY GAGA

The superstar artists from the 1980s have a worthy successor in the 21st century with the US singer Lady Gaga, who follows in the tradition of Madonna and combines glam rock and dance-pop with fashion, art and technology in highly produced stage performances. The fusion of genres mentioned at the start of this chapter is well represented by this talented performer. Lady Gaga takes her name from Queen's single 'Radio Ga Ga' (1984), and her debut album (*The Fame*, 2008) contained lyrics that concentrated on her wish to achieve fame and popularity.

MUSICAL EXAMPLE

LADY GAGA, 'JUST DANCE' (2008)

Lady Gaga

This upbeat dance number starts with a solo synthesiser riff featuring an unusual diminished 5th (between third and fourth quavers in the second bar):

which repeats, first with a chordal accompaniment, then with vocals and a syncopated quaver bass added.

0:15　The verse progresses in C♯ minor, in two-bar phrases with a bass line synth moving in syncopated quaver patterns for 16 bars until

0:48　the chorus is reached, still maintaining the key harmony with:

- C♯m E | G♯m/B B⁷sus⁴/F♯ :||
- and the melody line restricting its compass to within the octave, using E–C♯ as a hook on the word 'Dance' with timed delay echo.

1:07　Verse 2 is next, with different lyrics, followed by the chorus.

1:57　A middle section with guest male singer Colby O'Donis now provides a contrast, although the harmony and rhythm stay much the same.

2:28　Lady Gaga returns for another chorus and then

2:53　an unusual chromatic lead synthesiser solo is played for four bars over the repeated bass E leading to

3:01　a new two-part vocal with the parts hard panned left and right, featuring fast-moving rhymes set to descending note patterns over a rising octave bass ostinato reminiscent of a boogie woogie.

3:34　The chorus returns at first over the synth lead from the intro and the music ends with echoed descending minor 3rds to the song's title lyrics.

This is a retro, Madonna-influenced dance track with modern innovations, ideally suited to Lady Gaga's energetic stage shows.

DEVELOPMENTS IN MUSIC TECHNOLOGY

- The capabilities of computers and software for music increased.
- Virtual instrument plugins became more common than the real thing, with many vintage synthesisers and drum machines being emulated in software.
- The MP3 audio format became widely used. Audio compression formats had been in existence for some years but it wasn't until the 2000s that the quality and ease of use of MP3s had a real affect on the music business.
- In 2001 the Apple iPod and iTunes software were introduced.
- Broadband internet connection became fast enough for virtual jamming.
- There was a rise in away-from-home storage, with music uploaded to servers and shared on social networking sites, and sample libraries holding downloadable files (Napster, founded in 1999).
- High-definition (HD) audio and video become common, along with HD television (Freeview was launched in 2009).
- Mobile phone technology advanced enough to run music recording and sequencing software. Worldwide communications became much easier through text messaging and email.
- In 2010 the Apple iPad was introduced.

OVERVIEW: LOOKING BACK OVER THE DECADES

A number of common threads can be observed in pop music since the 1950s:

- *A growth in commercialism that drives forwards the production process.* Music reproduction and distribution have come a long way since the early days of Tin Pan Alley sheet-music publications. The music of vinyl records, CDs, and digital downloads brought into existence by engineers and producers combine with booking agents, promoters, business managers and entertainment lawyers, global advertising, publications, and online music stores to further the career of the would-be pop star. Live music has increased in importance since the beginning of the 21st century, having the advantage of a greater human presence and the element of risk that recorded music, which repeats exactly the same way every time, cannot provide. Nevertheless, live music is also supported by the commercial music industry through the stadium rock concert and growing numbers of outdoor festivals. There has been a noticeable decline in the traditional record industry's commercial outlets in recent years, with a decline in CD sales that threatens the viability of high-street stores, largely due to music on the internet.
- *Innovation and resourcefulness of the individual.* Despite the pressures of the mainstream record labels, and sometimes because of them, creative musicians have often held on tightly to their own musical values and been lauded by fans because of this. In the 21st century musicians can take control of the complete record-making process, writing their own material, recording it on sophisticated software on a home

computer and distributing the final result over the internet. This whole process allows them to maintain a degree of integrity that is sometimes very difficult to do when various stages are placed in the hands of others.

- *Developments in technology.* These have supported the creative imagination, and the fresh ideas of artists have spurred technology to new achievements. As computers have become more powerful so has the software written for them. The creation of music is ideally suited to the extensive control, processing and manipulation the software can provide as it is an art form that depends on developing material through repetition and evolution. It can allow human ideas to achieve their potential by removing technical and musical language barriers.

- *Rhythmical content employing subtleties of rhythm and dynamics, levels of which are not found in other genres with the exception of jazz.* It is difficult to explain in words exactly what the musical descriptors of 'swing', 'groove' or 'feel' mean, but these aspects of timing and relative loudness are key to all aspects of pop music, creating excitement and engaging the listener.

- *Music that is accessible to the general public.* The enjoyment that a listener obtains from listening to a pop record will spur them on to purchase the music in some form so that enjoyment can be replicated. This can also apply to instrumental dance tracks or more complex progressive compositions and classical music, but it is the pop song that dominates the commercial market. Vocal tracks have been by far the biggest sellers since the 1950s and look set to maintain their top position in years to come.

The musical elements

Progressions

Blues progression/12 bar 2, 12, 13
Cycle of 5ths 9, 67
50s progression 9, 22
Cadence 3, 14, 53, 122
Truck driver's modulation 21, 38
Tierce de Picardie 29
Tonic pedal 63
Modulation 104

Language

Diatonic 40, 102, 112
Chromatic 40, 55, 81, 100, 101
Discord 65, 108
Non-functional harmony 70
Suspensions 92

Rhythm

Speech rhythms 3
Syncopation 1, 12, 54, 55, 57, 65, 76, 104, 118, 123, 126, 128, 129
Dotted rhythm 14, 27, 60
Time signatures 22, 55, 56, 70, 71, 103

Cross-rhythms 24, 129
Shuffle rhythm 34, 60
Downbeats 22, 32
Backbeat 54
Offbeat 24, 28, 61, 69, 122, 124, 128, 129
Double-tempo 28

Form

12 bar blues structure 2, 3
AABA 9, 32
Solo break 7
Verse/chorus form 31
Simple verse form 34
Call and response 6, 7, 38
Transition 46
Suite 55
Bridge 66, 70, 76, 104, 117, 123, 124
Rondo 87
Tag 43, 87
Coda 24, 27, 28, 30, 43, 54, 63, 70, 75, 81, 85, 86, 90, 100, 102, 125

Index of musical examples

Index

Acknowledgements

The author and the publisher wish to thank the following copyright holders, without whose kind permission this book would not have been possible.

IMAGES

P13 Reproduced with permission from www.startdrumming.com
P24 Adapted from www.baswaphon.com.
P88 Horn section of Ojos de Brujo at concert in Espacio Movistar

All other pictures by Getty Images and Rex Features.

WORDS & MUSIC

(I'm Your) Hoochie Coochie Man
Words & Music by Willie Dixon
© Copyright 1957, 1985 Hoochie Coochie Music/Arc Music Corporation, USA.
Bug Music Limited (70%)/Jewel Music Publishing Company Limited (30%).
All Rights Reserved. International Copyright Secured.

What I'd Say
Words & Music by Ray Charles
© Copyright 1959 Progressive Music, USA.
Carlin Music Corporation.
All Rights Reserved. International Copyright Secured.

Hound Dog
Words & Music by Jerry Leiber & Mike Stoller
© Copyright 1956 Universal/MCA Music Limited (80%)/Chappell Morris Limited (20%).
All rights in Germany administered by Universal/MCA Music Publ. GmbH.
All Rights Reserved. International Copyright Secured.

Happy Birthday Sweet Sixteen
Words & Music by Howard Greenfield & Neil Sedaka
© Copyright 1961 Screen Gems-EMI Music Limited.
All Rights Reserved. International Copyright Secured.

Oh, Pretty Woman
Words & Music by Roy Orbison & Bill Dees
© Copyright 1964 (renewed 1992) Acuff